A WORK OF FAITH

A WORK OF FAITH

In Memory of Vera

JORGE FECUNDA
AND
VERA PALLARA

Library of Congress Control Number:		2019907352
ISBN:	Hardcover	978-1-9845-9033-6
	Softcover	978-1-9845-9035-0
	eBook	978-1-9845-9034-3

Print information available on the last page.

Rev. date: 06/13/2019

To order additional copies of this book, contact:
Xlibris
800-056-3182
www.Xlibrispublishing.co.uk
Orders@Xlibrispublishing.co.uk
797147

THE MINISTRY OF THE SEVEN LETTERS

(IL MINISTERO DELLE SETTE LETTERE)
ALL THE GLORY TO JESUS

In memory of Vera Pallara

This book will show an account of her life through her works of faith; done on this earth from 1999 to 2003 in cooperation with Jorge Fecunda.

-

TESTIMONIES

Testimonies of Vera' family and loved ones,
We Love & miss you ♡

Sarah Fecunda, Jacob Fecunda, Joy Fecunda- Vera's Kids

We love you, Ma, more than any words can ever express!
We live with your voice in us every day! (Sarah Fecunda, Jacob
Fecunda, Joy Fecunda)

Elena Pallara- Vera's sister

I shared with you my childhood, our laughter, our favorite
movies seen repeatedly, and your hand holding my hand when I was
afraid.

My adolescence, your advice, our first vacation, our first trip to
Greece, the two months in London, the concerts we went to see,
the decision to go and live in Bologna, our beers, our gin lemon,
our dances, and our chats until late at night, our laughter... We did
all this together.

Then we became adults, and we split up, you took your way,
and I took mine, you to London, me to Bologna and then my
return to Puglia, but despite the distance, we remained close, our
relationship remained indissoluble.

We kept hearing each other for everything, for every problem
you remained my adviser and how many laughs and how many you
and I also cried by phone, you always managed to cheer me up and
advise me, we could also laugh at our illnesses.

You didn't like to read that those who died of cancer didn't
make it, in fact, my sister, you made it for me.

You managed to make the life you wanted, your biggest dream was to travel the world and you did it!

You had three children you grew up with so much love, everyone who knew you remembers you as a special person because you were, and you will always be a special being.

I love you and I will always love you, for me you will always be my warrior♥

Rachele de Bonis, Vera's mom

Vera was a daughter that since childhood was a very clever girl. She always tried to do what she wanted. In fact, we had to enrol her in school a year earlier because she was always with a pen in hand, ready to copy the written pages of the newspapers. She also read to her father. Growing up, she never disappointed us—studying quietly in her room and calling us with enthusiasm each time she exceeded an exam. She has always been a strong girl. When she decided to do something, no one could even distract her, not even us her parents. She would discuss and always put forward her ideas. She decided to leave for London with her sister and did it, she decided to go live at Bologna and did it, she decided to travel the world with her husband and also did it, so I will simply say that my daughter has made the life she wanted, always loving closeness and distance. My daughter was my warrior. She endured this pain with a large force. She continued to play her life normally, even more enthusiastically. I was lucky enough to spend the last few months in London with her, and there were moments of joy thanks to her optimism. And like me, she was very religious. In fact, we always felt close to Him the closeness of Jesus. Vera, my first child, my first big love.

A CHAPTER OF VERA'S LIFE!

This story features her faith-work "the Ministry of the 7 Letters", and "Yes, We Believe Magazine". It also features her life lived as a mother, friend, wife and teacher. Essentially, she was a lover of life and everything life had to offer.

- **Everything comes to an end**...
  ...is a synopsis of what happened from 2002 to her passing 2019.

THE BIRTH OF JACOB AND THE END OF OUR SEVEN-LETTER MINISTRY

After Jacob was born, I realised that Vera hadn't finished her university degree; therefore, I brought it up in a conversation. Being the loving and cautious woman, she was, she asked me, 'How?' I simply replied, 'God will show us the way. Have faith.' With this, we went back to Macerata. Vera went on to complete her university degree in *lettera moderna* all whilst still being a mother, wife, and homemaker. Particularly, I recall the times she would wake up early to make fresh bread before hitting the books and looking after the children.

The struggle was real. Even though I had a job, pay was not great. We relied on supplies brought by my mother and father-in-law and of course, the grace of God. Although we had a complicated departure from Macerata, we were still filled with joy. Our next challenge was now to decide on where we could stay; we ended up settling at the home of Vera's parents. However, this was only temporary. You could almost say that this was a pit stop or a regroup for us to continue our journey. We had no clue where we were going. Only God knew.

Vera was an extraordinary woman, mother, and wife to me. We explored many countries, cities, and states, such as Holland, Eindhoven, New York, South Carolina, Miami, Curaçao, Germany, France, Spain, Israel, and London. Settling down was never easy for me, but she made it work for us; it was a blessing.

In London, she started her own personal journey to add more meaning to her life. She became a member of a parent group and then a lollipop lady who was loved by everyone. She later endeavoured on becoming a teaching assistant for age groups ranging from nursery to year 6 at Blessed Dominic Catholic Primary School. She successfully worked there until she became ill.

In memory of a wonderful journey with Vera, Veneranda Pallara, I would like to share with you a chapter in Vera's life that I can say I have had the privilege, honour, and joy to have had experienced with her and our kids—Sarah, Jacob, and Joy.

Like a true champion, she ran a race with us in this world, and now she has passed her baton over to us to continue her legacy, and so we shall in God's grace!

Vera departed on the 23 August 2018, and so I say, 'Eternal rest grant her, Lord. Shine Your perpetual light upon her. May she rest in peace now until all have been called to Your glorious resurrection. As it's written, when you died in Christ, you shall live in Christ. Amen.'

THE BIRTH OF OUR SON JACOB
by J. Fecunda

Thank You, Lord, for his arrival. Yes, great, he's Your first male. We have by faith declared him Yours, Jehovah Adonai, Jesus, and the Holy Spirit. Bless him, keep him, have Your will be done in his life, I pray. This, of course, is a surprise, but to us, everything has been told in advance to his name and that he was going to be a male! However, I must say, when told something by the Spirit and having to keep it to yourself is just very heavy, weighty, for people will test your faith and ask. Your answer need not be a lie! So how do you answer? I did it like this and told my wife to do the same. We said to those who asked us, 'Do you know what you will have? A boy or a girl?' Our answer was 'We'll have what God gives!'

Know truly that people ask things that truly need not be tampered with for it's in the hands of God Almighty if the baby lives or dies or if it's a boy or girl. It's a gift of the Lord God, as He says in the Bible that the children are a gift of God. So really, we just need to be grateful! In modern days, they can do a scan and tell you if you want, but there are also stories about the scan being inaccurate. So, for us, we stuck to the nature of some basic things. Remember, I said *we*, for we are not to judge, says the Lord! We all have opinions, and surely, out of 10 or 100 or 1,000 opinions of people, one can see God's consciousness and how it's different from the world's consciousness. So really, we should not to be the judges, but most of us do judge. We are happy, and if you have read the prayer of *Yes, We Believe Magazine* last month, we wrote his name already and thought we would have to let our readers know after, for it was hectic period. Well, I'm still not up to write much about this except that I'm happy and grateful to God, in the name of Jesus.

By V. Fecunda

I believe that when a child is born, we can say thanks only to God for this wonderful gift. As I wrote already in this magazine, the birth of a child is a miracle—a big and wonderful miracle of God. For nine months, there is already a baby present, and after this period, you can see a new life. A woman wants to be proud and say, 'I carried him/her for nine months. I felt the pain when he/she was born. No one can love him/her more than me.' Where is God in this thought? It's only thanks to God if the baby lives; it's only thanks to God if the baby grows. Yes, God uses us parents, but we cannot forget that God Almighty decides for the life of every human being. He lets us have our choice to do good or evil, so I believe that I cannot say to my children, 'Hey, I'm your mother, and you cannot understand how much I love you because I delivered you into this world.' No, I must say, 'Thank God for this life, for Your miracles. Thank You, God for these nine months of waiting and for the pain I suffered at the end. Thank You for these two wonderful gifts You gave us—Sarah and Jacob. We lift our children to You, Father Almighty. They are Your children, and no one can love them as You do. Thank You for choosing Jorge and me to be the parents of them. Amen.'

John

AUTHOR'S NOTE

After writing the seven letters, we shared our work on the street, praised and gave thanks to the Lord. "The Yes, We Believe magazine" concept started as an A3 paper; It was based on religious topics and topics close to our hearts. Essentially, it was a way of bringing our faith to life by expressing our creativity and spirituality in one medium. It is also important to note that we wanted the *"Yes, We Believe* magazine" to be released chronologically; we wanted to share the magazine to link to and remind people of the seven letters.

London n. 7 August 2002

FREE

MATTHEW 10: 8 "FREELY YOU HAVE RECEIVED, FREELY GIVE!"

YES, WE BELIEVE MAGAZINE

INTRODUCTION

This magazine will be based on 12 topics every month as we await arrival of our Saviour Jesus Christ. Walks of Jesus our Saviour as he lives through us with all his Glory, Sacrifices, Riches, Love, Ministry and Prayers. God bless you, as you take the time to see and read "Yes, We Believe Magazine!" It is unveil to those who are being saved. It is written simple and humble, and the Glory to Jesus.

Matthias

FOUNDER
JEHOVA ADONAI SHADDAI
JESUS CHRIST
THE HOLY SPIRIT
12 APOSTLES
ALL OF THE HOLY BIBLE THAT
WORK THROUGH US, YOUR
SERVANTS: JORGE, VENERANDA
& SARAH FECUNDA

FOR SUBSCRIPTION: fecundaj@hotmail.com

The beginning of our story is quite a simple one. Our main goal, I believe, was to share our love for God and build a family unit that we would provide and care for. The Ministry of the seven letters was our first and last faith project together; now that Vera is no longer here, in the flesh, I would like to share this chapter of her life with anyone who is willing to listen.

THE MINISTRY OF THE SEVEN LETTERS

In sharing this testimony, I seek not to have anyone pretend to be the judge of this story but leave this to the Lord God, who will judge all men! You are welcome to ask me questions, and yes, do your discernment.

I hope to encourage you in this manner, not to sin by judging!

We are all believers at one point in our life of knowing God. Through His mediator, Jesus Christ, we'll have a task or ministry!

Here is my testimony of how the Lord worked through mine. This, of course, will be in part! For as we live and uncover our motives, God Almighty has all the motives of man and will judge us all.

The writing of the seven letters happened after my rebirth! This testimony will have two parts. The first is after I'd been set apart for the Lord to educate me, as the Bible showed me later that God does this to those He chose! For it says in the book of John 6:45 NIV, 'It is written in the Prophets: They will all be taught by God. Everyone who listens to the Father and learns from him comes to me.'

I travelled from Holland to Israel and stayed there for a period of three months and then travelled to St Catharina for the journey through the mountains in Sinai. It's said that Mount Sinai is where Moses spoke and saw the glory of God as it passed by him.

In this period, because of my fasting and spiritual walk, I was challenged with depression, which is one of the attacks of the evil one on our search and conscious acceptance of Jesus. But praise God! He did not allow evil to win.

From this growth and challenge, I proceeded to Israel again for two months and a half, then after this to England with a short stop at Tenerife for a month, and then back to England to continue to Miami and then to Curaçao, where again I was challenged. This time, my biggest challenge was that even if I was born here in Curaçao, I always felt like I don't belong. I couldn't stand myself!

However, by this I'll remind the readers, Jesus was also not accepted in His own town. In saying this, I must say as well that Jesus is pure, and I wasn't, for this was to be done by the Spirit of Jesus by faith in coming back to the island and showing that Christ was working through me with more love. What a challenge! Because it's easy to show love to those you don't know! But I had to do it to those who already knew me and my efforts to walk in the light. It's written that a prophet is not accepted in his own town, as they have seen him grow and have a judgemental thought of him. Their unbelieving heart will say, 'Could this be possibly someone who God would work through? Who, Jesus? The son of the carpenter!' In my case, my name is Jorge, In this tale I know we all have a story; only some of us get to tell it by the blessing and perseverance of faith in God. The Lord prepares them to be the encouragement to those enlightened by their story.

The challenges on the island was so heavy that only faith in the Lord could have had me testifying to this today, because at one point the Bible quotes in the book of Matthew 12:43–45 NIV, 'When an evil spirit comes out of a man, it goes through arid places seeking rest and does not find it. Then it says, "I will return to the house I left." When it arrives, it finds the house unoccupied, swept clean, and put in order. Then it goes and takes with it seven other spirits more wicked than itself, and they go in and live there. And final condition of that man is worse than the first. That is how it will be with this wicked generation.'

When you haven't had the Lord come in and dwell in your temple (body), I knew I had. Anyhow, this is how the evil attacks to gain repossession of whom I have become—a man seeking righteousness and truth. The evil continued his attacks to the point of suicidal thoughts, which is not of God, so it was challenging! However, glory to Jesus, who is real for those who pray and call with all their might (heart, soul, mind, and body). Like the story of Jonah, the Lord hears and is faithful. He is an awesome God! Yes, He's there ready for us who like to quit or fly away. He's there, and He blesses when we call and repent truly.

Look at this: Jesus, who taught others to forgive seventy times seven, is basically telling us of His Father and our Father's mercy. Just imagine how often we have been unfaithful to God! I say truly repent and ask Him to guide you to a true repentance so that the Holy Spirit won't contemplate staying or coming and living in your temple (the man's body).

Well, this is what I did again after already having a rebirth. I said in a prayer: 'Father don't let my soul go to hell or to Satan. Please help me and show me that you will take me off of this island, for I have tried everything. And I know I serve you but can't take what was happening to me any longer, merciful Father. In the name of Jesus, I pray.' I guarantee to you that this is an example of the truth pray said; however, this is illustrated like this for writing the story for you, reader, with a bit more of words but get really the idea I have had it and went to my Creator in the name of the Master and Son. This is my point!

Okay, let's go to the Lord when we are in need, happy, or sick. Basically, let's go to the Creator. He is allowing this through the Son of His Holy Spirit, Jesus Christ.

Yes, there was something that I needed to do, such as staying in church and re-establishing my relationship with the Lord with a praycr prepared for me on the island by the guidance of the Holy Spirit and under submission of a pastor, J. Blundering of the Victory Outreach. I stayed and congregated with them and worked in the church. After many prayers and conduct of submission, the Lord heard me and did as I asked—only this time, He gave me a task that became the reason I am writing to you, reader, of this testimony of the seven letters. Only I did not know that it was going to take three years to write them and that this was also to be done with the help of a partner who was also responsible of confronting me with the truth of justice, love, and righteous action. In other words, not just as I want but in balance and to agree about anything we ask for (Matthew 18:19). So, this was His will for me leaving the island.

God is great and awesome! I left the island with my Bible, guitar, a box with the cassettes of the first spiritual recording done in Curaçao (Netherlands Antilles), a pair of pants, and two shirts—well, basically a small black backpack.

I have had my first stop in Italy, for I was to travel like Apostle Paul did, from Italy to Israel—Italy (Bologna to Bari), Greece (Athens), Israel (Haifa). Here I was stopped by the authority; by a miracle the Lord, I didn't have to pay the captain of the ship for the trip back to Athens. This all happened when I was travelling. All this with the revelations the Lord was giving me had been put together for the seven letters.

From Haifa (Israel) back to Athens and then to Italy, I encountered changes, challenges, and blessings; for I kept working, singing on the street, and proclaiming the name of the Messiah, Jesus Christ.

In Italy, I was blessed by the Lord when I meet a young man—Cesare was his name—who gave me a telephone number and said, 'I will get a room and fill it with +/− eight hundred people, and you can sing to them like you do here in Athens on the street.' I said, 'We'll see if God's willing.'

Through this action of my obedience of the Spirit, when I called, he asked me, 'Where are you?' And I said, 'In Bologna.' To make a long story short, that was where I was to find and start the journey with my partner. Today this blessing is my wife, Veneranda, that shortly after being in Italy and was about to continue my trip pilgrimage, ministry.

Veneranda at that time committed to the Lord to be with me, and we had confirmation of this by a pastor of an evangelical church that united us in the presence of the Holy Spirit, for this was a day of miracles in the church in Bologna.

Thanks to this unity, I completed my ministry of the seven letters. I thank You, God Almighty, for this. I know His anointing will be on whoever should read these letters, all of the Holy Scriptures. How they were linked together can only be the Lord of miracle and mystery, for I'm like a string. There is a sound or action when the Lord plays me,

All this testimony is true in faith as it's written to encourage us believers, and I believe that His intent was that now through the church, the manifold wisdom of God should be made known to the rulers and authorities in the heavenly realms, which He accomplished in Christ Jesus, our Lord.

I hope and pray that our letters also touch and heal those of little or no belief if and when they read this humble story of faith of having a ministry of our great God Almighty that really doesn't need me!

Hallelujah! May the grace of the Lord Jesus Christ fill each one of us. To the glory and praises of His holy name. Amen!

FIRST SPIRITUAL LETTER

Dear children, let us not love with words or tongue but with actions and in truth.

Love keeps no record of wrong, it does not delight in evil but rejoices with the truth.

It always protects, always trusts, always hopes, always perseveres. I tell you: love your enemies and pray for those who persecute you, that you may be sons of your Father in heaven.

He causes his sun to rise on the evil and the good and sends rain on the righteous and the unrighteous. Love must be sincere. Hate what is evil; cling to what is good.

Be devoted to one another in brotherly love. Honour one another above yourselves.

Never be lacking in zeal, but keep your spiritual fervour, serving the Lord.

Be joyful in hope, patient in affliction, faithful in prayer. Share with God people who are in need.

Practise hospitality. Bless those who persecute you; bless and do not curse.

Rejoice with those who rejoice; mourn with those who mourn. Live in harmony with one another.

Do not be proud but be willing to associate with people of low position. Do not be conceited.

Do not repay anyone evil for evil. Be careful to do what is right in the eyes of everybody.

If it is possible, as far as it depends on you, live at peace with everyone.

Do not take revenge my friends, but leave room for God's wrath, for it is written: 'It is mine to avenge; I will repay,' says the Lord.

On the contrary: 'If your enemy is hungry, feed him. If he is thirsty, give him something to drink. In doing this, you will heap burning coals on his head.'

Do not be overcome by evil but overcome evil with good.

Glory to Jesus!

1 John 3:18; 1 Corinthians 13:6–7; Matthew 5:44–45; Romans 12:9–21

SECOND SPIRITUAL LETTER

Therefore, there is now no condemnation for those who are in Christ Jesus, because through Christ Jesus the law of the Spirit of life set me free from the law of sin and death.

Those who live according to the sinful nature have their minds set on what that nature desires; but those who live in accordance with the spirit have their minds set on what the spirit desires.

And the Lord God said, 'The man has now become like one of us, knowing good and evil. He must not be allowed to reach out his hand take also from the tree of life and eat and live forever.'

But Christ has indeed been raised from the dead, the first fruits of those who have fallen asleep. For since death came through a man, the resurrection of the dead comes also through a man.

For as in Adam all die, so in Christ all will be made alive. But each in his own turn: Christ, the first fruits; then, when he comes, those who belong to him. You, however, are controlled not by the sinful nature but by the spirit, if the spirit of God lives in you. And if anyone does not have the spirit of Christ, he does not belong to Christ. Those controlled by the sinful nature cannot please God. So, God created man in his own image, in the image of God he created him; male and female he created them.

Now if we are children, then we are heirs, heirs of God and co-heirs with Christ, if indeed we share in his sufferings in order that we may also share in his glory.

Jesus called God his own father, making himself equal with God. The Spirit himself testifies with our spirit that we are God's children. Come back to your senses as you ought and stop sinning; for there are some who are ignorant of God. I say this to your shame.

See, you are well again, stop sinning or something worse may happen to you.

I tell you the truth, a time is coming and has now come when the dead will hear the voice of the Son of God and those who hear will live.

I know you are Abraham's descendants. Yet you are ready to kill me, because you have no room for my word. Jesus said to them, 'If God were your father, you would love me, for I came from God and now am here. I have not come on my own; but he sent me. The world cannot hate you, but it hates me because I testify that what it does is evil.'

For you did not receive a spirit that makes you a slave again to fear, but you received the Spirit of sonship. And by him we cry, 'ABBA, FATHER.'

And if the Spirit of him who raised Jesus from the dead is living in you, he who raised Christ from the dead will also give life to your mortal bodies through his Spirit, who lives in you.

And if Christ has not been raised, our preaching is useless and so your faith. More than that, we are then found to be false witnesses about God, for we have testified about God that he raised Christ from the dead.

But he did not raise him if in fact the dead are not raised. But if Christ is in you, your body is dead because of sin, yet your spirit is alive because of righteousness.

Therefore brothers, we have an obligation, but is not to the sinful nature, to live according to it. For if you live according to the sinful nature, you will die; but if by the Spirit you put the death the misdeeds of the body, you will live.

The mind of sinful man is death, but the mind controlled by the Spirit is life and peace, because those who are led by the Spirit of God are sons of God.

The sinful mind is hostile to God. It does not submit to God's law, nor can it do so.

For what the law was powerless to do in that it was weakened by the sinful nature, God did by sending his own son in the likeness of sinful man to be a sin offering.

And so, he condemned sin in sinful man, in order that the righteous requirements of the law might be fully met in us, who do not live according to the sinful nature but according to the Spirit.

Glory to Jesus!

Romans 8:1–2, 5; Genesis 3:22; 1 Corinthians 15:20–23; Romans 8:9, 8; Genesis 1:27; Romans 8:17; John 5:18; Romans 8:16; 1 Corinthians 15:34; John 5:14, 25; 8:37, 42; 7:7; Romans 8:15, 11; 1 Corinthians 15:14–15; Romans 8:10, 12–13, 6, 14, 7, 3–4

THIRD SPIRITUAL LETTER

The King will reply, 'I tell you the truth, whatever you did for one of the least of these brothers of mine, you did for me.'

Yours sons have fainted; they lie at the head of every street, like antelope caught in a net.

They are filled with the wrath of the Lord and the rebuke of your God.

Therefore, hear this, you afflicted one, made drunk, but not with wine. This is what your sovereign Lord says, your God, who defends his people: 'See, I have taken out of your hand the cup that made you stagger; from that cup, the goblet of my wrath, you will never drink again.' 'I will put it into the hands of your tormentors, who said to you fall prostrate that we may walk over you, and you made your back like the ground, like a street to be walked over.'

For this is what the sovereign Lord says: 'At first my people went down to Egypt to live; lately, Assyria has oppressed them. And now what do I have here?' declares the Lord. 'For my people have been take away for nothing, and those who rule them mock' declares the Lord. 'And all day long my name is constantly blasphemed. Therefore, my people will know my name; therefore, in that day they will know that it is I who foretold it. Yes, it is I.'

For this is what the Lord says: 'You were sold for nothing, and without money you will be redeemed.'

I tell you the truth, anyone who gives you a cup of water in my name because you belong to Christ will certainly not lose his reward.

He who is kind to the poor lends to the Lord, and he will reward him for what he has done.

He who oppresses the poor shows contempt for their maker, but whoever is kind to the needy honours God.

God is not unjust; he will not forget your work and the love you have shown him as you have helped his people and continue to help them.

Glory to Jesus!

Matthew 25:40; Isaiah 51:20–23; 52:4–6, 3; Mark 9:41; Proverbs 19:17; 14:31; Hebrews 6:10

FOURTH SPIRITUAL LETTER

It is right for me to feel this way about all of you, since I have you in my heart; for whether I'm in chains or defending and confirming the gospel, all of you share in God's grace with me.

So that you may be able to discern what is best and may be pure and blameless until the day of Christ, filled with the fruit of righteousness that comes through Jesus Christ, to the glory and praise of God.

And the Lord God said: 'The man has now become like one of us, knowing good and evil. He must not be allowed to reach out his hand and take also from the tree of life and eat, and lives for ever.'

Being confident of this that he who began a good work in you will carry it on to completion until the day of Christ Jesus.

Glory to Jesus!

Philippians 1:7, 10–11; Genesis 3:22; Philippians 1:6

FIFTH SPIRITUAL LETTER

Some men brought to him a paralytic, lying on a mat. When Jesus saw their faith, he said to the paralytic, 'Take hearth, son; your sins are forgiven.' Jesus Christ is the same yesterday and today and for ever. As a result, he does not live the rest of his earthly life for evil human desires, but rather for the will of God.

And so, Jesus also suffered outside the city gate to make the people holy through his own blood. Let us, then, go to him outside the camp, bearing the disgrace he bore.

And he died for all, that those who live should no longer live for themselves but for him who died for them and was raised again.

For here we do not have an enduring city; but we are looking for the city that is to come.

Keep on loving each other as brothers. Do not forget to entertain strangers, for by so doing some people have entertained angels without knowing it.

And do not forget to do good and to share with others, for with such sacrifices God is pleased.

Remember those in prison as if you were their fellow-prisoners, and those who are ill-treated as if you yourselves were suffering.

Marriage should be honoured by all, and the marriage bed kept pure, for God will judge the adulterer and all the sexually immoral.

Keep your lives free from the love of money and be content with what you have, because God has said, 'Never will I leave you; never I will forsake you.'

So, we say with confidence, 'The Lord is my helper; I will not be afraid. What can man do to me?'

Don't you know that when you offer yourselves to someone to obey him as slaves, you are slaves to the one whom you obey, whether you are slaves to sin, which leads to death, or to obedience, which leads to righteousness?

Do not be carried away by all kinds of strange teachings. It is good for our hearts to be strengthened by grace, not by ceremonial foods, which are of no value to those who eat them.

Remember your leaders, who spoke the word of God to you. Consider the outcome of their way of life and imitate their faith.

Obey your leaders and submit to their authority. They keep watch over you as men who must give an account. Obey them so that their work will be a joy, not a burden, for that would be of no advantage to you.

I have been crucified with Christ and I no longer live, but Christ lives in me. The life I live in the body, I live by faith in the Son of God, who loved me and gave himself for me.

In the same way, count yourselves dead to sin but alive to God in Christ Jesus. Therefore, do not let sin reign in your mortal body so that you obey its evil desires. Do not offer the parts of your body to sin, as instruments of wickedness, but rather offer yourselves to God, as those who have been brought from death to life; and offer the parts of your body to him as instruments of righteousness.

Because our gospel came to you not simply with words, but also with power, with the Holy Spirit and with deep conviction. You know how we lived among you for your sake. For sin shall not be your master, because you are not under law, but under grace.

Finally, be strong in the Lord and in his mighty power. Therefore, put on the full armour of God, so that when the day of evil comes, you may be able to stand your ground, and after you have done everything, to stand. Stand firm then, with the belt of truth buckled round your waist, with the breastplate of righteousness in place, and with your feet fitted with the readiness that comes from the gospel of peace.

In addition to all this, take up the shield of faith, with which you can extinguish all the flaming arrows of the evil one.

Take the helmet of salvation and the sword of the Spirit, which is the word of God. And pray in the Spirit on all occasions with all kinds of prayers and requests.

May the God of peace, who trough the blood of eternal covenant who brought back from the dead our Lord Jesus, that great Shepherd of the sheep, equip you with everything good for doing his will, and may he work in us what is pleasing to him, through Jesus Christ, to whom be glory for ever and ever. Amen

Glory to Jesus!

Matthew 9:2; Hebrews 13:8; 1 Peter 4:2; Hebrews 13:12–13; 2 Corinthians 5:15; Hebrews 13:14, 1, 2, 16, 3–6; Romans 6:16; Hebrews 13:9, 7, 17; Galatians 2:4; Hebrews 13:18; Galatians 2:20; Romans 6:11, 13; 1 Thessalonians 1:5; Romans 6:14; Ephesians 6:10, 13–18; Hebrews 13:20, 21

SIXTH LETTER

The wall of the city had twelve foundations, and on them were the names of the twelve apostles of the Lamb.

Do you not know that he who unites himself with a prostitute is one with her in body? For it is said, 'The two will become one flesh.' But he who unites himself with the Lord is one with him in spirit.

Flee from sexual immorality. All other sins a man commits are outside his body, but he who sins sexually sins against his own body.

Do you not know that your body is a temple of the Holy Spirit, who is in you, whom you have received from God? You are not your own; you were bought at a price. Therefore, honour God with your body.

In the beginning God created the heavens and the earth. Now the earth was formless and empty, darkness was over the surface of the deep, and the Spirit of God was hovering over the waters.

Brothers, I could not address you as spiritual but as worldly—mere infants in Christ. I gave you milk, not solid food, for you were not yet ready for it. Indeed, you are still not ready. You are still worldly. For since there is jealousy and quarrelling among you, are you not worldly? Are you not acting like mere men? For when one says, 'I follow Paul', and another, 'I follow Apollo', are you not mere men?

Blessed is the one who reads the words of this prophecy and blessed are those who hear it and take to heart what is written in it, because the time is near.

Don't grumble against each other, brothers, or you will be judged. The Judge is standing at the door!

Brothers, as an example of patience in the face of suffering, take the prophets who spoke in the name of the Lord.

Therefore, say to the house of Israel, this is what the Sovereign LORD says: Repent! Turn from your idols and renounce all your detestable practices!

When any Israelite or any alien living in Israel separates himself from me and sets up idols in his heart and puts a wicked stumbling block before his face and then goes to a prophet to inquire of me, I the LORD will answer him myself.

We know that anyone born of God does not continue to sin; the one who was born of God keeps him safe, and the evil one cannot harm him. We know that we are children of God, and that the whole world is under the control of the evil one. We know also that the Son of God has come and has given us understanding, so that we may know him who is true. And we are in him who is true—even in his Son, Jesus Christ. He is the true God and eternal life.

Dear children, keep yourselves from idols. Therefore, prepare your minds for action; be self-controlled; set your hope fully on the grace to be given you when Jesus Christ is revealed. As obedient children do not conform to the evil desires you had when you lived in ignorance. But just as he who called you is holy, so be holy in all you do; for it is written: 'Be holy, because I am holy.'

Unlike so many, we do not peddle the word of God for profit. On the contrary, in Christ we speak before God with sincerity, like men sent from God.

Dear friends, do not believe every spirit, but test the spirits to see whether they are from God, because many false prophets have gone out into the world. This is how you can recognize the Spirit of God: Every spirit that acknowledges that Jesus Christ has come in the flesh is from God, but every spirit that does not acknowledge Jesus is not from God. This is the spirit of the antichrist, which you have heard is coming and even now is already in the world.

You, dear children, are from God and have overcome them, because the one who is in you is greater than the one who is in the world. They are from the world and therefore speak from the viewpoint of the world, and the world listens to them. We are from God, and whoever knows God listens to us; but whoever is not from God does not listen to us. This is how we recognize the Spirit of truth and the spirit of falsehood.

For, 'Everyone who calls on the name of the Lord will be saved.' How, then, can they call on the one they have not believed in? And how can they believe in the one of whom they have not heard? And how can they hear without someone preaching to them? And how can they preach unless they are sent? As it is written, 'How beautiful are the feet of those who bring good news!'

Don't you know that you yourselves are God's temple and that God's Spirit lives in you? If anyone destroys God's temple, God will destroy him; for God's temple is sacred, and you are that temple.

Do not deceive yourselves. If any one of you thinks he is wise by the standards of this age, he should become a 'fool' so that he may become wise. For the wisdom of this world is foolishness in God's sight. As it is written: 'He catches the wise in their craftiness'; and again, 'The Lord knows that the thoughts of the wise are futile.'

For who makes you different from anyone else? What do you have that you did not receive? And if you did receive it, why do you boast as though you did not?

Already you have all you want! Already you have become rich! You have become kings—and that without us! How I wish that you really had become kings so that we might be kings with you! For it seems to me that God has put us apostles on display at the end of the procession, like men condemned to die in the arena. We have been made a spectacle to the whole universe, to angels as well as to men. We are fools for Christ, but you are so wise in Christ! We are weak, but you are strong! You are honoured, we are dishonoured! To this very hour we go hungry and thirsty, we are in rags, we are brutally treated, and we are homeless. We work hard with our own hands. When we are cursed, we bless; when we are persecuted, we endure it; when we are slandered, we answer kindly. Up to this moment we have become the scum of the earth, the refuse of the world.

Dear friends, let us love one another, for love comes from God. Everyone who loves has been born of God and knows God. Whoever does not love does not know God, because God is love. We know that we live in him and he in us, because he has given us of his Spirit. And we have seen and testify that the Father has sent his Son to be the Saviour of the world.

No one can come to me unless the Father who sent me draws him, and I will raise him up at the last day. It is written in the

Prophets: 'They will all be taught by God.' Everyone who listens to the Father and learns from him comes to me. No one has seen the Father except the one who is from God; only he has seen the Father. I tell you the truth, he who believes has everlasting life. I am the bread of life. Your forefathers ate the manna in the desert, yet they died. But here is the bread that comes down from heaven, which a man may eat and not die. The Spirit gives life; the flesh counts for nothing. The words I have spoken to you are spirit and they are life. Yet there are some of you who do not believe. For Jesus had known from the beginning which of them did not believe and who would betray him. He went on to say, 'This is why I told you that no one can come to me unless the Father has enabled him.'

Whoever claims to live in him must walk as Jesus did. If we claim we have not sinned, we make him out to be a liar and his word has no place in our lives.

The reason I wrote you was to see if you would stand the test and be obedient in everything.

If you forgive anyone, I also forgive him. And what I have forgiven—if there was anything to forgive—I have forgiven in the sight of Christ for your sake, in order that Satan might not outwit us. For we are not unaware of his schemes.

But I have a mind as well as you; I am not inferior to you. Who does not know all these things?

Let him who does wrong continue to do wrong; let him who is vile continue to be vile; let him who does right continue to do right; and let him who is holy continue to be holy.

Jesus answered: Watch out that no one deceives you. For many will come in my name, claiming, I am the Christ, and will deceive many. You will hear of wars and rumours of wars but see to it that you are not alarmed. Such things must happen, but the end is still to come. Nation will rise against nation, and kingdom against kingdom. There will be famines and earthquakes in various places. All these are the beginning of birth pains.

Then you will be handed over to be persecuted and put to death, and you will be hated by all nations because of me. At that time many will turn away from the faith and will betray and hate each other, and many false prophets will appear and deceive many people. Because of the increase of wickedness, the love of most will grow cold, but he who stands firm to the end will be saved. And this gospel of the kingdom will be preached in the whole world as a testimony to all nations, and then the end will come.

So, when you see standing in the holy place 'the abomination that causes desolation,' spoken of through the prophet Daniel, let the reader understand.

He will confirm a covenant with many for one 'seven.' In the middle of the 'seven' he will put an end to sacrifice and offering. And on a wing of the temple he will set up an abomination that causes desolation, until the end that is decreed is poured out on him.

They will bear their guilt-the prophet will be as guilty as the one who consults him.

Do not love the world or anything in the world. If anyone loves the world, the love of the Father is not in him. For everything in the world—the cravings of sinful man, the lust of his eyes and the boasting of what he has and does—comes not from the Father but from the world. The world and its desires pass away, but the man who does the will of God lives forever.

Be patient, then, brothers, until the Lord's coming. See how the farmer waits for the land to yield its valuable crop and how patient he is for the autumn and spring rains. You too, be patient and stand firm, because the Lord's coming is near.

Outside are the dogs, those who practice magic arts, the sexually immoral, the murderers, the idolaters and everyone who loves and practices falsehood.

As you know, we consider blessed those who have persevered. You have heard of Job's perseverance and have seen what the Lord finally brought about. The Lord is full of compassion and mercy.

Since you call on a Father who judges each man's work impartially, live your lives as strangers here in reverent fear.

By standing firm, you will gain life.

Glory to Jesus!

Revelation 21:14; 1 Corinthians 6:16–20; Genesis 1:1–2; 1 Corinthians 3:1–4; Revelation 1:3; James 5:9–10; Ezekiel 14:6–7; 1 John 5:18–21; 1 Peter 1:13–16; 2 Corinthians 2:17; 1 John 4:1–6; Romans 10:13–15; 1 Corinthians 3:16–20; 4:10, 9, 11–13, 7, 8; 1 John 4:7, 8, 13–14; 6:44–50, 63–65; 2:6; 1:10; 2 Corinthians 2:10–11, 9; Job 12:3; Revelation 22:11; Matthew 24:4–15; Daniel 9:27; Ezekiel 14:10; 1 John 2:15–17; James 5:7–8; Revelation 22:15; James 5:11; 1 Peter 1:17; Luke 21:19

SEVENTH SPIRITUAL LETTER

And do this, understanding the present time. The hour has come for you to wake up from your slumber, because our salvation is nearer now than when we first believed. The night is nearly over; the day is almost here. So let us put aside the deeds of darkness and put on the armour of light.

Put to death, therefore, whatever belongs to your earthly nature: sexual immorality, impurity, lust, evil desires and greed, which is idolatry. Because of these, the wrath of God is coming. You used to walk in these ways, in the life you once lived. But now you must rid yourselves of all such things as these: anger, rage, malice, slander, and filthy language from your lips. Do not lie to each other, since you have taken off your old self with its practices and have put on the new self, which is being renewed in knowledge in the image of its Creator.

Therefore, since we are God's offspring, we should not think that the divine being is like gold or silver or stone—an image made by man's design and skill. In the past God overlooked such ignorance, but now he commands all people everywhere to repent. For he has set a day when he will judge the world with justice by the man he has appointed. He has given proof of this to all men by raising him from the dead.

What business is it of mine to judge those outside the church? Are you not to judge those inside? God will judge those outside. 'Expel the wicked man from among you.'

Do not work for food that spoils, but for food that endures to eternal life, which the Son of Man will give you. On him God the Father has placed his seal of approval.

Jesus answered, 'The work of God is this: to believe in the one he has sent.'

Then Jesus declared, 'I am the bread of life. He who comes to me will never go hungry, and he who believes in me will never be thirsty. But as I told you, you have seen me and still you do not believe. For I have come down from heaven not to do my will but to do the will of him who sent me. And this is the will of him who sent me, that I shall lose none of all that he has given me but raise them up at the last day. The Spirit gives life; the flesh counts for nothing. The words I have spoken to you are spirit and they are life. Yet there are some of you who do not believe.' For Jesus had known from the beginning which of them did not believe and who would betray him.

For what I received I passed on to you as of first importance: that Christ died for our sins according to the Scriptures, that he was buried, that he was raised on the third day according to the Scriptures, and that he appeared to Peter, and then to the Twelve. After that, he appeared to more than five hundred of the brothers at the same time, most of whom are still living, though some have fallen asleep.

Then I saw another angel flying in mid-air, and he had the eternal gospel to proclaim to those who live on the earth, to every nation, tribe, language and people. He said in a loud voice, 'Fear God and give him glory, because the hour of his judgment has come. Worship him who made the heavens, the earth, the sea and the springs of water.'

A second angel followed and said, 'Fallen! Fallen is Babylon the Great, which made all the nations drink the maddening wine of her adulteries.'

A third angel followed them and said in a loud voice: If anyone worships the beast and his image and receives his mark on the forehead or on the hand, he, too, will drink of the wine of God's fury, which has been poured full strength into the cup of his wrath. He will be tormented with burning sulphur in the presence of the holy angels and of the Lamb. This calls for patient endurance on the part of the saints who obey God's commandments and remain faithful to Jesus.

Then I heard a voice from heaven say, 'Write: Blessed are the dead who die in the Lord from now on.'

'Yes,' says the Spirit, 'they will rest from their labour, for their deeds will follow them.'

For the grace of God that brings salvation has appeared to all men. It teaches us to say 'No' to ungodliness and worldly passions, and to live self-controlled, upright and godly lives in this present age, while we wait for the blessed hope—the glorious appearing of our great God and Saviour, Jesus Christ.

But now in Christ Jesus you who once were far away have been brought near through the blood of Christ, the Counsellor, the Holy Spirit, whom the Father will send in my name, will teach you all things and will remind you of everything I have said to you.

He who descended is the very one who ascended higher than all the heavens, in order to fill the whole universe.) It was he who gave some to be apostles, some to be prophets, some to be evangelists, and some to be pastors and teachers, to prepare God's people for works of service, so that the body of Christ may be built up until we all reach unity in the faith and in the knowledge of the Son of God and become mature, attaining to the whole measure of the fullness of Christ.

Jesus answered, 'My teaching is not my own. It comes from him who sent me. If anyone chooses to do God's will, he will find out whether my teaching comes from God or whether I speak on my own. He who speaks on his own does so to gain honour for himself, but he who works for the honour of the one who sent him is a man of truth; there is nothing false about him. Has not Moses given you the law? Yet not one of you keeps the law. Why are you trying to kill me?'

Love does not delight in evil but rejoices with the truth. It always protects, always trusts, always hopes, and always perseveres.

Love never fails. But where there are prophecies, they will cease; where there are tongues, they will be stilled; where there is knowledge, it will pass away. For we know in part and we prophesy in part, but when perfection comes, the imperfect disappears. When I was a child, I talked like a child, I thought like a child, I reasoned like a child. When I became a man, I put childish ways behind me. Now we see but a poor reflection as in a mirror; then we shall see face to face. Now I know in part; then I shall know fully, even as I am fully known.

And now these three remain: faith, hope and love. But the greatest of these is love.

I have revealed you to those whom you gave me out of the world. They were yours; you gave them to me and they have obeyed your word. Now they know that everything you have given me comes from you. For I gave them the words you gave me and they accepted them. They knew with certainty that I came from you, and they believed that you sent me. I pray for them. I am not praying for the world, but for those you have given me, for they are yours. All I have is yours, and all you have is mine. And glory has come to me through them.

If anyone speaks in a tongue, two—or at the most three—should speak, one at a time, and someone must interpret. If there is no interpreter, the speaker should keep quiet in the church and speak to himself and God.

Two or three prophets should speak, and the others should weigh carefully what is said. And if a revelation comes to someone who is sitting down, the first speaker should stop. For you can all prophesy in turn so that everyone may be instructed and encouraged. For God is not a God of disorder but of peace.

As in all the congregations of the saints, women should remain silent in the churches. They are not allowed to speak, but must be in submission, as the Law says. If they want to inquire about something, they should ask their own husbands at home; for it is disgraceful for a woman to speak in the church. But everything should be done in a fitting and orderly way.

Rejoice in the Lord always. I will say it again: Rejoice! Let your gentleness be evident to all. The Lord is near. Do not be anxious about anything, but in everything, by prayer and petition, with thanksgiving, present your requests to God. And the peace of God, which transcends all understanding, will guard your hearts and your minds in Christ Jesus.

Finally, brothers, whatever is true, whatever is noble, whatever is right, whatever is pure, whatever is lovely, whatever is admirable—if anything is excellent or praiseworthy—think about such things. Whatever you have learned or received or heard from me or seen in me—put it into practice. And the God of peace will be with you.

My prayer is not that you take them out of the world but that you protect them from the evil one.

My prayer is not for them alone. I pray also for those who will believe in me through their message, that all of them may be one, Father, just as you are in me and I am in you. May they also be in us so that the world may believe that you have sent me.

I pray that you may be active in sharing your faith, so that you will have a full understanding of every good thing we have in Christ.

For we are to God the aroma of Christ among those who are being saved and those who are perishing. To the one we are the smell of death; to the other, the fragrance of life. And who is equal to such a task?

You show that you are a letter from Christ, the result of our ministry, written not with ink but with the Spirit of the living God, not on tablets of stone but on tablets of human hearts. He has made us competent as ministers of a new covenant—not of the letter but of the Spirit; for the letter kills, but the Spirit gives life.

The God of this age has blinded the minds of unbelievers, so that they cannot see the light of the gospel of the glory of Christ, who is the image of God. For we do not preach ourselves, but Jesus Christ as Lord, and ourselves as your servants for Jesus' sake. For God, who said, 'Let light shine out of darkness', made his light shine in our hearts to give us the light of the knowledge of the glory of God in the face of Christ.

But we have this treasure in jars of clay to show that this all-surpassing power is from God and not from us. We are hard pressed on every side, but not crushed; perplexed, but not in despair, persecuted, but not abandoned; struck down, but not destroyed.

It is written: 'I believed; therefore, I have spoken.'

With that same spirit of faith, we also believe and therefore speak, so we fix our eyes not on what is seen, but on what is unseen. For what is seen is temporary, but what is unseen is eternal.

If we have been united with him like this in his death, we will certainly also be united with him in his resurrection.

Now if we died with Christ, we believe that we will also live with him.

Therefore, since we have been justified through faith, we have peace with God through our Lord Jesus Christ, through whom we have gained access by faith into this grace in which we now stand. And we rejoice in the hope of the glory of God. Not only so, but we also rejoice in our sufferings, because we know that suffering produces perseverance; perseverance, character; and character, hope. And hope does not disappoint us, because God has poured out his love into our hearts by the Holy Spirit, whom he has given us.

His intent was that now, through the church, the manifold wisdom of God should be made known to the rulers and authorities in the heavenly realms, according to his eternal purpose which he accomplished in Christ Jesus our Lord. In him and through faith in him we may approach God with freedom and confidence. I ask you, therefore, not to be discouraged because of my sufferings for you, which are your glory. I pray that out of his glorious riches he may strengthen you with power through his Spirit in your inner being, but in your hearts set apart Christ as Lord.

Always be prepared to give an answer to everyone who asks you to give the reason for the hope that you have. But do this with gentleness and respect, keeping a clear conscience, so that those who speak maliciously against your good behavior in Christ may be ashamed of their slander.

Glory to Jesus!

Romans 13:11–12; Colossians 3:5–10; Acts 17:29–31; 1 Corinthians 5:12–13; John 6:29, 27, 35–36, 38–39, 63–64; 1 Corinthians 15:3–6; Revelation 14:6–10, 12–13; Titus 2:11–13; Ephesians 2:13; John 14:26; Ephesians 4:10–13; John 7:16–19; 1 Corinthians 13:6–13; John 17:6–10; 1 Corinthians 14:31, 33–35, 27–30, 40; Philippians 4:9; John 17:15, 20–21; Philemon 6; 2 Corinthians 2:15–16; 3:6, 3; 4:13, 8–9, 18, 4–7; Romans 6:5, 8; 5:1–5; Ephesians 3:10–13, 16; 1 Peter 3:15–16

London N. 0 (Inauguration) January 2002

Freely you have received, freely give! (Matthew 10:8 NIV)

YES, WE BELIEVE MAGAZINE!

INTRODUCTION

Peter

This magazine will be based on twelve topics every month as we await the arrival of our Saviour, Jesus Christ. Walk with Jesus, our Saviour, as He lives through us with all His glory, sacrifices, riches, love, ministry, and prayer. God bless you as you take the time to see and read *Yes, We Believe Magazine!* It is unveiled to those who are being saved. It is written simply and humbly. All the glory to Jesus.

John

EVANGELISING IN THE STREET

Who is it for? Everyone.

How is it done? By confessing and proclaiming the name of Jesus.

And why? This is ours to do when we believe and accept Jesus as Lord and Saviour (Matthew 28:19–20).

How do we do it? We do it by singing on the streets. If you can imagine passing by and hearing on a corner glory to Jesus, by the grace that through belief and faith is being manifested through the presence of the Lord.

This is healing, comforting, blessing, and many other things that, through testimony, we will keep you informed until one day we meet (James 1:18–19).

In the UK—places where we've glorified the Lord Jesus by praising.

James

FIRST SPIRITUAL LETTER

Dear children, let us not love with words or tongue but with actions and in truth.

Love keeps no record of wrong, it does not delight in evil but rejoices with the truth.

It always protects, always trusts, always hopes, always perseveres.

I tell you: love your enemies and pray for those who persecute you, that you may be sons of your father in haven.

He causes his sun to rise on the evil and the good and sends rain on the righteous and the unrighteous.

Love must be sincere. Hate what is evil; cling to what is good.

Be devoted to one another in brotherly love. Honor one another above yourselves.

Never be lacking in zeal, but keep your spiritual fervor, serving the Lord.

Be joyful in hope, patient in affliction faithful in prayer. Share with God people who are in need.

Practice hospitality. Bless those who persecute you; bless and do not curse.

Rejoice with those who rejoice; mourn with those who mourn. Live in harmony with one another.

Do not be proud but be willing to associate with people of low position. Do not be conceited.

Do not repay anyone evil for evil. Be careful to do what is right in the eyes of everybody. If it is possible, as far as it depends on you, live at peace with everyone.

Do not take revenge my friends, but leave room for God's wrath, for it is written: "it is mine to avenge; I will repay," says the Lord.

On the contrary: "if your enemy is hungry, feed him. If he is thirsty, give him something to drink. In doing this, you will keep burning coals on his head".

Do not be overcome by evil but overcome evil with good.

GLORY TO JESUS

1 John 3:18; 1 Corinthians 13:6-7; Matthew 5:44-45; Romans 12:9-21.

Andrew

MY TESTIMONY
by J. Fecunda

My testimony is that God is true to those who seek Him honestly and earnestly will know Jesus. Like it's written in the Bible, for the sin of one man, there is reconciliation through one man and that is Jesus. Bible Quote: Romans 5:17.

I had a rebirth in a period where I needed guidance of the right way!

So through a friend I was brought closer to a believers congregation, where after a few visit I accepted the Spirit of Jesus, which than set me apart for the growth and ministry I now have which is only through Faith and Grace. I'm held strong in Christ Jesus.

I say, when the Spirit of Jesus is guiding, you'll know by your daily walk. You become conscious of what is of God or of the world.

Repent and Live.

Glory to Jesus.

Ezekiel 18:32 NIV "For I take no pleasure in death of anyone, declares the Sovereign Lord Repent and live!"

So I Thank You Jesus.

Bartholomew

IT'S ARRIVED—THE TABERNACLE OF THE LORD

As by faith, we have this calling today, and I'm happy to announce the tabernacle of our faith in Jesus, our Lord and Saviour, of whom was spoken of from the beginning of time and all through the Scriptures old and new. They spoke of Him coming back for us believers of Him!

In the Old Testament, it is written 1 Chronicles 6:31–32 NIV, 'These are the men David put in charge of the music in the house of the Lord after the ark came to rest there. They ministered with music before the tabernacle, the Tent of Meeting, until Solomon built the temple of the Lord in Jerusalem. They performed their duties according to the regulations laid down for them.' And in the New Testament, in Acts 15:16–18 NIV, 'After this I will return and rebuild David's fallen Tabernacle its ruins I will rebuild, and I will restore it, that the remnant of men may seek the Lord, who does these things that have been known for ages.' Every month by the first, where the Spirit of Jesus leads us, we will set up in and by faith the tabernacle of the Lord to bless those who are in sight and those in that area. We believe up to 12.000 km from where we stand, people who are honestly seeking the Lord, the Holy Spirit, will receive, in the name of Jesus Christ. Amen

> The point of what we are saying is this: We do have such a high priest, who sat down at the right hand of the throne of the Majesty in heaven, and who serves in the sanctuary, the true tabernacle set up by the Lord, not by man. (Hebrews 8:1–2 NIV)

Philip

OPINION ON THIS QUESTION
by J. Fecunda

<u>Why do you not have a organization or pastor of a church to send you or to guide you? Or to Whom do you submit?</u>

First of all our organization is the Kingdom of God by faith, belief and conduct of life in our Master Jesus. He's our Shepherd. We all believers have one pastor and that is Jesus. <u>Who guides me?</u> The Spirit of God like it's written in the Bible "And the Spirit of God was hovering over the waters" Genesis 1: 1,2

To whom do we submit? To the Holy Spirit 1 Corinthians 2:10 "but God has revealed it to us by his Spirit. The Spirit searches all things of God.

Hebrews 12:9 NIV "Moreover, we have all had human fathers who disciplined us and we respected them for it, how much more should we submit to the father of our Spirit and Live!

For Kids

TUTU, PRINCESS OF GOD
ADVENTURES WITH TUTU

Thomas

Who is Tutu?

Tutu is a lovely little girl.

She is only eleven months old.

She already had many adventures in many different parts of the world.

She flew with so much joy eight times and went to Italy, Holland, USA, and the Caribbean. She was born here in London.

She sings in the street with Daddy and Mummy (I know that now you, readers, are thinking, *It is impossible. She is only eleven months old. She cannot sing.* I mean, she makes sounds like *Aaaaaaaaaa!* For me, this is a beautiful sound by God. And when she is at home, she likes to dance, clap her hands, sing, and play the tambourine.

Tutu is only eleven months old, but her life is already completely dedicated to Jesus Christ, our Saviour.

For this reason, she is so happy.

(To be continued next month, in the name of Jesus.)

Matthew

OUR JOURNEY WITH JESUS
by Vera Pallara Fecunda

Dear Sarah,

You came into our life eleven months ago. That day, God gave us a beautiful and wonderful gift—you, princess of God. The first time I met your father, I spoke so much to him, and we danced an Italian folk dance. We were so embarassed.

I remember everything we spoke of that night. He showed to me tranquillity and a strong faith in Jesus. In that period, I did not know Jesus like now and I did not know anything about the power of the Holy Spirit and how He can work through His servant.

From that night, my life started to change . . .
(To be continued next month, in the name of Jesus.)

NEWS FROM THE HOLY BIBLE

The Beatitudes

Now when he saw the crowds, he went up on a mountainside and sat down.

His disciples came to him, and he began to teach them saying:

Blessed are the poor in spirit, for theirs is the kingdom of heaven.

Blessed are those who mourn, for they will be comforted.

Blessed are the meek, for they will inherit the earth.

Blessed are those who hunger and thirst for righteousness, for they will be filled.

Blessed are the merciful, for they will be shown mercy.

Blessed are the pure in heart, for they will see God.

Blessed are the peacemakers, for they will be call sons of God.

Blessed are those who are persecuted because of righteousness, for theirs is the kingdom of heaven.

Blessed are you when people insult you, persecute you and say all kinds of evil against you because of me.

Rejoice and be glad, because great is your reward in heaven, for in the same way they persecuted the prophets who were before you.

Matthew 5:1–12 NIV

Simon

MY TRUTH ABOUT MY CHRISTIAN LIFE
by Vera Pallara Fecunda

I don't believe in the many different churches.
We have the same Master and Saviour—Jesus Christ.

Matthias

People to pray for:

- Ryan and family
- Jobcentre and its workers
- Davide, bass player from Italy
- Luca Ronca and Rachele Atzei
- Maggi family
- Pallara family
- Tucker family
- Fecunda family
- My immediate circle

If you know how to pray this, then please do!

If you don't know and wish to, do this prayer:

'Jesus, I believe You are the Son of God who raised again and lived in the consciousness of man to teach and help us our redemption and salvation. Holy Spirit of Jesus, You are welcome in my temple [mind, body, and soul]. I will consider this done. Thank You, in the name of Jesus. Amen.'

After this, just consider this a call made to Jesus and say, 'Please help my brothers [call the names written].'

Founder:
Jehovah Adonai Shaddai
Jesus Christ
Holy Spirit
12 Apostoles
All the Holy Bible that worked through us your servants: Jorge, Vera, and Sarah Fecunda

YES, WE BELIEVE MAGAZINE!

Email address: fecundaj@hotmail.com (If you want to subscribe, you can reach us through this email.)

London N. 1 February 2002

Freely you have received, freely give! (Matthew 10:8 NIV)

YES, WE BELIEVE MAGAZINE!

INTRODUCTION

Peter

This magazine will be based on twelve topics every month as we await the arrival of our Saviour, Jesus Christ. Walk with Jesus, our Saviour, as He lives through us with all His glory, sacrifices, riches, love, ministry, and prayer. God bless you as you take the time to see and read *Yes, We Believe Magazine!* It is unveiled to those who are being saved. It is written simply and humbly. All the glory to Jesus.

John

EVANGELISING IN THE STREET

Who is it for?

Everyone

How is it done?

By confessing and proclaiming the name of Jesus.

And why?

This is ours to do when we believe and accept Jesus as Lord and Saviour.

Matthew 28: 19, 20.

How do we do it?

We do it by singing on the streets, if you can imagine passing by and hearing on a corner Glory to Jesus, by the grace that through belief and faith is being manifested through the presence of the Lord. This is healing, comforting, blessing and many other things that through testimony, we will keep you informed until one day we meet.

James 1: 18, 19

When we think of evangelising, it can have many forms. Consider this form as I give this testimony: We were on our way to Brixton and took the bus, in the bus route 211, from Hammersmith to Victoria. This time of the day, it was full. So a man saw my wife, Veneranda, and our daughter, Sarah, who was almost one year. He got up so they can sit.

I did not know what was going to happen next. He did a kind deed which led to us talking in the bus. Reader, if you can imagine for twenty minutes or plus we spoke. This man, eighty-three years old, teaching five-year-old children at school, shared his story with me in the bus. The Bible says in Genesis 5:1–2, 'When God created man, he made him in the likeness of God, He created them male and female and blessed them, and when they were created, He call them Man.'

What is my point? We are in the likeness, but how much of this consciousness is in us daily?

Well, this man, eighty-three years old, had a need to express himself, which made evangelising easy for me. Evangelising has the spiritual aspect of 'LET THE SPIRIT LEAD'. When we understand this, the Bible confirms this in Genesis 1:2, 'Before there was anything the Spirit of God Almighty was hovering over the waters.'

Further, we learn from the King of Kings, through his teachings. In the Bible, it is written, 'For there is one God and one mediator between God and men, the man Christ Jesus, who gave himself as a ransom for all man, the testimony given in it's proper time' (1 Timothy 2:5).

So to evangelise, we need to let the Spirit guide very important. Why? Because Jesus saved us not because of the righteous things we had done but because of his mercy. He saved us through the washing of rebirth and renewal by the Holy Spirit.

The testimony of evangelism ends with this kind man receiving a cassette, a gift which confesses and proclaims Jesus, our Saviour. He was happy to receive the gift. In the bus, there was a nice feeling of everyone being part of this graceful happening, another seed that God will take care of, for God was pleased in him.

Yes, glory to Jesus!

James

FIRST SPIRITUAL LETTER

Dear children, let us not love with words or tongue but with actions and in truth.

>Love keeps no record of wrong, it does not delight in evil but rejoices with the truth. It always protects, always trusts, always hopes, always preseveres. I tell tou: love your enemies and pray for those who persecute you, that you may be sons of your father in haven. He causes his sun to rise on the evil and the good and sends rain on the righteous and the unrighteous. Love must be sincere. Hate what is evil; cling to what is good.

Be devoted to one another in brotherly love. Honour one another above yourselves.

Never be lacking in zeal, but keep your spiritual fervour, serving the Lord.

Be joyful in hope, patient in affliction faithful in prayer. Share with God people who are in need. Practise hospitality. Bless those who persecute you; bless and do not curse.

Rejoice with those who rejoice; mourn with those who mourn. Live in harmony with one another. Do not be proud, but be willing to associate with people of low position. Do not be conceited. Do not repay anyone evil for evil. Be careful to do what is right in the eyes of everybody. If it is possible, as far as it depends on you, live at peace with everyone.

Do not take revenge my friends, but leave room for God's wrath, for it is written: "it is mine to avenge; i will repay", says the Lord. On the contrary: "if your enemy is hungry, feed him. If he is thirsty, give him something to drink. In doing this, you will keap burning coals on his head".

Do not be overcome by evil, but overcome evil with good.

GLORY TO JESUS

1 John 3:18; 1 NIV Corinthians 13:6-7 NIV;
Matthew 5:44-45 NIV; Romans 12:9-21 NIV.

Freely you have received, freely give! (Matthew 10:8 NIV)

Andrew

OPINION ON THIS QUESTION
by J. Fecunda

Why do you not have a organization or pastor of a church to send you or to guide you? Or to Whom do you submit?

First of all our organization is the Kingdom of God by faith, belief and conduct of life in our Master Jesus. He's our Shepherd. We all believers have one pastor and that is Jesus. *Who guides me?* The Spirit of God like it's written in the Bible "And the Spirit of God who was hovering over the waters" Genesis 1: 1, 2

To whom do we submit? To the Holy Spirit 1 Corinthians 2:10 NIV "but God has revealed it to us by his Spirit. The Spirit searches all things of God.

Hebrews 12:9 NIV "More over, we have all had human fathers who disciplined us and we respected them for it, how much more should we submit to the father of our Spirit and Live!

Why do you believe in God?

Because of my personal relationship with Him in me!

I'm 40 years old and have done my share of questioning and seeking and doing, there are many theories, science and concept of which if you choose one of them you'll have to believe! "Right", When I do my homework or research, I will still have to believe. So God has proven to be the choice for me! That why I believe in God, for God is in me. How much of God? Depends on me, becoming more and more conscious of God in me and Jesus opens up this more when I learned more about Him.

What do you think of the Churches?

What about churches?

Is God in the Churches.

Yes, Genesis 3:22 teaches us believers that God created man, "And now the man has become like one of us" I would ask How much of God?

Because there is also written "knowing good and evil."

Philip

MY TESTIMONY
by J. Fecunda

My testimony is that God is true to those who seek Him honestly and earnestly will know Jesus. Like it's written in the Bible, for the sin of one man, there is reconciliation through one man and that is Jesus. <u>Bible Quote:</u> Romans 5:17.

I had a rebirth in a period where I needed guidance to go the right way!

So through a friend, I was brought closer to a believers congregation, where after a few visit I accepted the Spirit of Jesus, which than set me apart for the growth and ministry I now have which is only through Faith and Grace.

I'm held strong in Christ Jesus.

I say, when the Spirit of Jesus is guiding, you'll know by your daily walk. You become conscious of what is of God or of the world.

Repent and Live.

Glory to Jesus.

Ezekiel 18:32 NIV 'For I take no pleasure in death of anyone, declares the Sovereign Lord Repent and live!'

So I Thank You Jesus.

Bartholomew

IT'S ARRIVED—THE TABERNACLE OF THE LORD

As by faith we have this calling today I'm happy to announce the Tabernacle of our faith in Jesus, our Lord and Saviour of who, was spoken of from the beginning of time and all trough the Scripture old and new, they spoke of him coming back for us believers in Him!

In the Old Testament is written 1 Chronicles 6: 31, 32 NIV 'These are the men David put in charge of the music in the house of the Lord after the ark came to rest there. They ministered with music before the tabernacle, the Tent of Meeting, until Solomon built the temple of the Lord in Jerusalem. They performed their duties according to the regulations laid down for them.' and in the New Testament in Acts 15: 16, 18 NIV 'After this I will return and rebuild David's fallen Tabernacle its ruins I will rebuild, and I will restore it, that the remnant of men may seek the Lord, who does these things that have been known for ages. Every month by the 1st where the Spirit of Jesus leads us, we will set up in and by faith the Tabernacle of the Lord to bless those who are in sight and those in that area. We believe up to 12.000 km from where we stand, people who are honestly seeking the Lord, Holy Spirit will receive in the name of Jesus Christ.

Amen

Thank You, Lord, for we began by grace Your tabernacle and had already seen what You can do when we walk in faith.

We started, and one man sitting ten meters from us in the park of Shepherd's Bush Green got up and came closer after a few songs and our praising.

Thank You, Jesus, for the Spirit.

About half an hour later, there were four men sitting next to one another on the bench, and two were talking to each other.

The praising was loud. One asked for a request, and I have got the opportunity to say who we are and that our faith in Christ Jesus is what has been manifested and that today, 1 January 2002, is the inauguration of the tabernacle of the Lord. And God willing, we will do this every month where the Spirit takes us.

So I said, 'I'm sorry for the song that I did not know, because all the songs I know are mine, and they are biblical and spiritual songs to praise and glorify the Lord, in the name of Jesus.' And I said to him, 'If you want, I will improvise by letting the Spirit lead me, and you can sing.' So he said yes and got up and grabbed the microphone and sang. Patrik, I believe was from Ireland, and his friend sang.

I praised and thanked God while they sang. I believe the song Shoan sang was Irish folk, and Patrik sang 'Oh Lord, It's Hard to Be Humble'. As we said in our prayer, the tabernacle is to do just what happened on 1 January 2002. May the man seek God and repent so the Holy Spirit can lead us through until the Lord's coming. At that point, we left them with a cassette that glorifies Jesus. Thank You, Jesus, for Shoan, Patrik, Harold, and our 12.000 km of faith that heals and restores and frees the captives by the grace of the Holy Spirit.

> The point of what we are saying is this: We do have such a high priest, who sat down at the right hand of the throne of the Majesty in heaven, and who serves in the sanctuary, the true tabernacle set up by the Lord, not by man. (Hebrews 8:1 NIV)

Thomas

For Kids

TUTU, PRINCESS OF GOD

Who is Tutu?

Tutu is a Lovely little girl.

She is only 11 months old.

She had already many adventure in many different parts of the world.

She flew with so much joy, 8 times and went to Italy, Holland, U.S.A and Caribean and she was born here in London.

She sings in the street with daddy and mummy (I know that now you, reader are thinking 'It is impossible she is only 11 months old, she cannot sing' I mean she makes sounds like: 'AAAAABBA' and for me this is a beatiful sound to GOD. When she is at home she likes to dance, clap her hands, sing and play the tamburine. Tutu is only 11 months old but her life is already completely dedicate to Jesus Christ our Saviour.

For this reason she is so happy.

(to be continued next month in the name of Jesus)

NEWS FROM THE HOLY BIBLE (MIAMI ITALY)

THE HOLY BIBLE

The Beatitudes

Matthew 5:1-12 NIV

Now when he saw the crowds, he went up on a mountainside and sat down.

His disciples came to him, and he began to teach them saying: blessed are the poor in spirit, for theirs is the kingdom of heaven.

Blessed are those who mourn, for they will be comforted.

Blessed are the meek, for they will inherit the earth. Blessed are those who hunger and thirst for righteousness, for they will be filled.

Blessed are the merciful, for they will be shown mercy.

Blessed are the pure in heart, for they will see God.

Blessed are the peacemakers, for they will be call sons of God.

Blessed are those who are persecuted because of righteousness, for theirs is the kingdom of heaven.

Blessed are you when people insult you, persecute you and say all kinds of evil against you because of me.

Rejoice and be glad, because great is your reward in heaven, for in the same way they persecuted the prophets who were before you.

James

The Law and the Prophets were proclaimed until John. Since that time, the good news of the kingdom of God is being preched and every one is forcing his way into it.

Luke 16:16 NIV

Simon

MY TRUTH ABOUT MY CHRISTIAN LIFE
by V. Pallara Fecunda

I don't believe in the many different churches.
We have the same Master and Saviour—Jesus Christ.

Matthias

People to pray for:

  - Philip the Evangelist
  - Steve and Sarah
  - Patrik from Ireland
  - Shoan
  - Harold
  - MTB Bologna
  - Cesare and M. Grazia
  - Elena and her dog (Pablo)
  - Bambina
  - Ryan and family
  - Jobcenter and its workers
  - Davide, bass player
  - Luca and Rachele
  - Maggi family
  - Pallara family
  - Marcello and Ingrid
  - Gennifer Garbier
  - Lucinda and family
  - My immediate circle

If you know how to pray this, then please do!
If you don't know and wish to pray, do this prayer:

'Jesus, I believe You are the Son of God who raised again and lived in the consciousness of man to teach and help us on our redemtion and salvation.

Holy Spirit of Jesus, You are welcome in my temple [mind, body, and soul]. I will consider this done. Thank You, in the name of Jesus. Amen.

After this, just consider this a call made to Jesus and say, "Please help my brothers [call the names written].'

Judas or Thaddaeus

OUR JOURNEY WITH JESUS
by V. Pallara Fecunda

Dear Sarah,

you came in our life 11 months ago, God gave us that day a beatiful and wonderful gift, you, princess of God. The first time I met your father i spoke so much to him and we danced a folk italian dance, we were so embarassed.

I remember that everithing we spoke of that night, he showed to me a tranquillity and strong faith in Jesus. In that period I did not know Jesus like now and I did not know nothing about the power of the Holy Spirit and how He can work through his servant.

From that night my life started to change.........................
(to be continued next month in the name of Jesus)

Founder:
Jehovah Adonai Shaddai
Jesus Christ
Holy Spirit
12 Apostoles
All the Holy Bible that worked through us your servants: Jorge, Veneranda, and Sarah Fecunda

YES, WE BELIEVE MAGAZINE!

Sponsor: Fecunda family, www.sailmiami.com

If you want to subscribe, you can through this email address: fecundaj@hotmail.com.

London N. 2 March 2002

Freely you have received, freely give! (Matthew 10:8 NIV)

YES, WE BELIEVE MAGAZINE!

INTRODUCTION

Peter

This magazine will be based on twelve topics every month as we await the arrival of our Saviour, Jesus Christ. Walk with Jesus, our Saviour, as He lives through us with all His glory, sacrifices, riches, love, ministry, and prayer. God bless you as you take the time to see and read *Yes, We Believe Magazine!* It is unveiled to those who are being saved. It is written simply and humbly. All the glory to Jesus.

John

Joel 2:28, 29 NIV

And afterwards, I will pour out my Spirit on all people. Your sons and daughters will prophesy, your old men will dream dreams, your young men will see visions. Even on my servants, both men and women, I will pour out my Spirit in those days.

James

SECOND SPIRITUAL LETTER

Therefore, there is now no condemnation for those who are in Christ Jesus, because through Christ Jesus the law of the Spirit of life set me free from the law of sin and death. Those who live according to the sinful nature have their minds set on what that nature desires; but those who live in accordance with the spirit have their minds set on what the spirit desires. And the Lord God said, "the man has now become like one of us, knowing good and evil. He must not be allowed to reach out his hand take also from the tree of life and eat, and live for ever". But Christ has indeed been raised from the dead, the firstfruits of those who have fallen asleep. For since death came through a man, the resurrection of the dead comes also through a man. For as in Adam all die, so in Christ all will be made alive. But each in his own turn: Christ, the firstfruits; then, when he comes, those who belong to him. You, however are controlled not by the sinful nature but by the spirit, if the spirit of God lives in you. And if anyone does not have the spirit of Christ, he does not belong to Christ. Those controlled by the sinful nature cannot please God. So God created man in his own image, in the image of God he created him; male and female he created them. Now if we are children, then we are heirs, heirs of God and co-heirs with Christ, if indeed we share in his sufferings in order that we may also share in his glory. Jesus called God his own father, making himself equal with God. The Spirit himself testifies with our spirit that we are God's children.

Come back to your senses as you ought and stop sinning; for there are some who are ignorant of God. I say this to your shame. See, you are well again, stop sinning or something whorse may happen to you. I tell you the truth, a time is coming and has now come when the dead will hear the voice of the son of God and those who hear will live. I know you are Abraham's descendants. Yet you are ready to kill me, because you have no room for my word. Jesus said to them, "if God were your father, you would love me, for I came from God and now am here. I have not come on my own; but he sent me. The world cannot hate you, but it hates me because i testify that what it does is evil. For you did not receive a spirit that makes you a slave again to fear, but you received the Spirit of sonship. And by him we cry, "ABBA, FATHER". And if the Spirit of him who raised Jesus from the dead is living in you, he who raised Christ from the dead will also give life to your mortal bodies through his Spirit, who lives in you. And if Christ has not been raised, our preaching is useless and so your faith. More than that, we are then found to be false witnesses about God, for we have testified about God that he raised Christ from the dead. But he did not raise him if in fact the dead are not raised. But if Christ is in you, your body is dead because of sin, yet your spirit is alive because of righteousness. Therefore brothers, we have an obligation, but is not to the sinful nature, to live according to it. For if you live according to the sinful nature, you will die; but if by the Spirit you put the death the misdeeds of the body, you will live. The mind of sinful man is death, but the mind controlled by the Spirit is life and peace, because those who are led by the Spirit of God are sons of God. The sinful mind is hostile to God. It does not submit to God's law, nor can it do so. For what the law was powerless to do in that it was weakened by the sinful nature, God did by sending his own son in the likeness of sinful man to be a sin offering. And so he condemned sin in sinful man, in order that the righteous requirements of the law might be fully met in us, who do not live according to the sinful nature but according to the Spirit.

GLORY TO JESUS

ROMANS 8:1,2,5; GENESIS 3:22; 1 CORINTHIANS 15:20-23; ROMANS 8:9,8;
GENESIS 1:27; ROMANS 8:17; JOHN 5:18; ROMANS 8:16; 1 CORINTHIANS 15:34;
JOHN 5:14, 25; JOHN 8:37, 42; JOHN 7:7; ROMANS 8:15, 11; 1 CORINTHIANS 15: 14, 15; ROMANS 8:10,12,13,6,14,7,3,4

Andrew

OPINION ON THIS QUESTION
by J. Fecunda

What do you think about the different Christian religions? It's clear that one needs to see in this question that the man's ego is at work in him, and only God will judge this! I see no need in dividing one man or his teaching. Saying this, we will have to accept that *religion* is a complicated word for we all are religious in breathing God's air, without refraining one another from doing this with freedom. And when it comes to Christ, He said to love one another, so when this is being accomplished other religions or people preaching the Word of God this is understandable because is written until we all reach the fullness in faith in Christ Jesus. I say oke, yes, let them not fool people but preach Jesus Christ as we all believers will do by the love we have for our Saviour. Amen!

Jesus spoke about submission to one another. Peter and Paul spoke also about submission of the woman to her husband. What do you think about this?

Yes, Jesus spoke and showed submission to one another. My opinion is that only trough submission can we see God at work in us. The evil is seen and understood because of not being able to submit. In other words, when you know God, your submission is in effect, and when you don't, you reject the submission. For this reason, we have all things like rebellion, disagreement, etc. You know, because we all human beings have been rebellious at one stage in our life. Christ Jesus, as we learn of Him, had never been rebellious with God and submitted Himself to the Almighty for He came from Him. This purpose is to show that this can be done when all generations of men have not understood submission. He came in the flesh to do just this so that the Scriptures can be fullfilled.

Let's all praise *Jesus*!

Hebrews 3:10–13

Psalm 8

Thank You, *Jesus*!

Psalm 13

Malachi 1:2–5

When I say I belive

In the morning

Who can say

I wanna welcome

Moving with the Holy Spirit

The joy in Christ

Look at Christ

Tune hallelujah

Jesus, I like thinking of you

Just a minute

Bartholomew

TUTU, PRINCESS OF GOD

When Tutu went for the first time to Miami, she was only four months old. She arrived to Miami from New York after a long travel of twenty-four hours in the bus. In Miami, every day she was with her father and mother on the street to praise God, and she met many people, like her friends Curtis and Sunny. After two weeks, she left Miami, and for four days, she slept at MIA (Miami Airport). She was so happy to have a house so big like MIA. In this big house, she danced like a princess for the first time with her father in a big hall. God is good, and after four days, He gave to Tutu and her family a free ticket for Curaçao so they could continue they travel to bring the good news of Jesus Christ to all people.

(To be continued next month, in the name of Jesus.)

Thomas

NEWS FROM THE BIBLE

[1]The Spirit clearly says that in later times some will abandon the faith and follow deceiving spirits and things taught by demons. [2]Such teachings come through hypocritical liars, whose consciences have been seared as with a hot iron. [3]They forbid people to marry and order them to abstain from certain foods, which God created to be received with thanksgiving by those who believe and who know the truth. [4]For everything God created is good, and nothing is to be rejected if it is received with thanksgiving, [5]because it is consecrated by the word of God and prayer.

[6]If you point these things out to the brothers, you will be a good minister of Christ Jesus, brought up in the truths of the faith and of the good teaching that you have followed. [7]Have nothing to do with godless myths and old wives' tales; rather, train yourself to be godly. [8]For physical training is of some value, but godliness has value for all things, holding promise for both the present life and the life to come.

[9]This is a trustworthy saying that deserves full acceptance [10](and for this we labour and strive), that we have put our hope in the living God, who is the Saviour of all men, and especially of those who believe.

[11]Command and teach these things. [12]Don't let anyone look down on you because you are young, but set an example for the believers in speech, in life, in love, in faith and in purity. [13]Until I come, devote yourself to the public reading of Scripture, to preaching and to teaching. [14]Do not neglect your gift, which was given you through a prophetic message when the body of elders laid their hands on you.

[15]Be diligent in these matters; give yourself wholly to them, so that everyone may see your progress. [16]Watch your life and doctrine

closely. Persevere in them, because if you do, you will save both yourself and your hearers.

1 Timothy 4 NIV

THE STORY OF TUTU PRINCESS OF GOD

Philip

AND AS YOU SING PSALMS, HYMNS, AND SPIRITUAL SONGS WITH GRATITUDE IN HEART TO GOD

We have already mention to the readers of *Yes, We Believe Magazine* in so many words that through evangelising, story of a cassette been given as the last exchange with person who accepted our faith in Jesus. Today I want to say a little bit of why I have a cassette. For nine years already, the Lord had been working on having me ready for this day as I'm confessing and talking of the greatness of the Lord, which we all individually have a story. Our God is an awesome god! After my rebirth in the Spirit of Jesus, I started changing the words of the songs I used to sing, putting or pleasing His name for more consciousness, and this helped my growth of staying focused. And this I have done all through my travels with the guitar, as someone who sang to glorify Jesus on the street or wherever I was asked to play. My introduction of myself was always this: 'I sing spiritual songs if this is okay with you, for I'm singing for Jesus.' People always had the choice—when I was not singing on the street but in places like bars, restaurants, kibbutz (Israel), weddings, discotheques, for children, hospitals, mental houses, etc.—to say no to my singing. Obviously, my songs are about Jesus and confronting as they are mostly biblical words, psalms, and so on. I say 'I sing for the joy of the Lord.' On 3 May 1999, a cassette by the grace of our Lord Jesus in spiritual action was recorded; 5,000 copies had been given to people—some as gifts, some in exchange for money. This was depending on where in the world I was, for example: Italy, £7.000; Greece, 700 drachma; Holland, 7 guilders; Israel, 7 shekels; England, 1 or 3 pounds; Curaçao, 7 Ant. guilders; America, for fifty cassettes and to continue my trip, I was given 700 dollars.

But the cassette is also in places where I have not been as yet, like Australia, New Zealand, Korea, Japan, and Alaska. Since God has blessed us with a CD this time, that is a continuation of the work of the Lord by faith in singing songs and sharing consciousness in the ministry that I have. With the cassette, I did not know what the Lord had installed for me, because I was with the Holy Spirit and my guitar. Now when you hear the CD, you'll hear my daughter, Sarah, and my wife, Veneranda (Vera), and more conviction of my ministry of faith in our Lord Jesus Christ. When you want a copy of either cassette or CD, do not hesitate to ask and you shall receive! Reach us via email: fecundaj@hotmail.com.

God bless you!

Matthew

THE TABERNACLE

The first of February was a strange day. If you have read the first issue of *Yes, We Believe Magazine*, you know already that every first of the month, by faith, we do the tabernacle. In February, we have done this in Brook Green Park. I remember that day was raining, and it was cold. I thought, *How can we do this? We have to praise God in a park, but it's raining.* My husband said, 'Don't worry. It's important that we start. Maybe we will do only one song, as God wants.' When we started, the rain stopped, and we could sing for one and a half hour. A strong wind was with us, for me, for my faith was the presence of the Holy Spirit because for one and a half hour, I was not cold, and the sensation of this wind was so beautiful. We do not stop the people while we are praising God. God is freedom, and Jesus, if I understood from the Scriptures, did not stop no one. So when someone stops, it's because the Spirit has communicated with them to stop. So to conclude, I can say that day I saw a miracle. God protected us from the rain, from the cold, and He gave us so much joy and healing. I saw this in me, my husband, and my daughter. And I have faith that in 12.000 km, everyone has been comforted, healed, and received the Spirit of our Lord Jesus, because faith is being sure of what we hope for and certain of what we do not see.

James

MY TRUTH ABOUT MY CHRISTIAN LIFE
by V. Pallara Fecunda

Love, yes, Jesus said, 'Love one another.' When I met Jorge, my husband, I had my concept of love; and when I started the relationship with him, I thought, *I really love this man.* Day after day, step by step, I understood more about love. The love that Jesus taught us is patient, kind, it does not envy, it does not boast, it is not proud, it is not rude, it is not self-seeking, it is not easily angered, it keeps no record of wrongs; love does not delight in evil but rejoice with the truth. It always protects, always trusts, always hopes, always perseveres (1 Corinthians 13:4–7). Yes, I know many things, and I have learnt many things about the love of Jesus, but I have to confess to everyone who is reading this magazine (because God Almighty knows already) that sometimes it's so difficult because of my ego. The ego in me gives me another interpretation of love: 'First of all, love yourself.' Many times I thought, *I'm not egoistic.* It's not the truth, because the ego in me makes me egoistic, and only the voice of God in us can submit the evil (ego) in us. To conclude, in John 15:12 NIV, Jesus said, 'My command is this: Love each other as I have loved you.'

Simon

OUR JOURNEY WITH JESUS
by V. Pallara Fecunda

Dear Sarah,

This month I wrote to you a short story. I hope you can understand everything. God bless you, in the name of Jesus. I will write in Italian, and I'll make a little translation in Enlgish.

C'era una volta un grosso uccello, a cui piaceva volare alto, tanto alto, e viaggiava da un paese all'altro conoscendo cosi' tanti altri uccelli. La sua grande gioia era lodare il suo Creatore che l'aveva benedetto con una voce piu' bella di qualsiasi altro uccello. Un giorno il grande uccello in uno dei suoi viaggi, incontra un piccolo uccello abbattuto, cosi' abbattuto che non aveva neanche piu' le penne con cui coprirsi. Il piccolo uccello rimase colpito dalla forza e dalla bellezza del grande uccello e gli disse: "Sai grande uccello, io non so volare pero' sento di poterlo fare con te", il piccolo uccello non sapeva che il suo problema non era il non saper volare, il problema era un piccolo anello con catena attaccato a una delle sue zampine, che lo teneva legato alla terra, lei non si era mai accorta di questo ma il grande uccello, con la saggezza che Dio li dava, lo aveva subito notato e quando il piccolo uccello li chiese di poter volare con lui, si preoccupo' un po' perche' lui era gia' pronto per un nuovo grande volo e sapeva che volaeva aiutare il piccolo uccello doveva restare un altro po' sulla terra. Decise di farlo, pensando: "OK! Dio mi dara' la forza di spezzare questo anello cosi' lei potra' volare, con me o senza di me non e' importante perche' io dopo questo continuero' il mio volo. Non e' la prima volta che un uccello piccolo come questo mi chiede aiuto". Dopo i primi piccoliu passi, il piccolo uccello era felice, aveva un po' paura ma, aveva cosi' tanta gioia di poter essere con il grande uccello che lodava con tanto amore il suo Creatore. Un bel giorno, il piccolo uccello si accorse dell' anello ed ebbe paura, tanta paura che senti' l'anello stringersi ancor piu' forte alla sua zampina e proprio in quel momento il Grande uccello li stava dicendo: "Ehi, non preoccuparti io posso darti una piccola chiave che ti liberera'!" Ma, il piccolo uccello continuava ad aver paura e sentiva la catena dell' anello.

(To be continued next month, in the name of Jesus.)

People to pray for:

- Stefano
- Simona and the newborn
- Mr Itaru and his wife
- Roberto Bologna Alan
- Netti, Lisa, and the newborn
- Mr Capello
- Mr Stanley

If you know how to pray this, then please do!
If you don't know and wish to pray, do this prayer:
'Jesus, I believe You are the Son of God who raised again and lived in the consciousness of man to teach and help us on our redemtion and salvation.

Holy Spirit of Jesus, You are welcome in my temple [mind, body, and soul]. I will consider this done. Thank You, in the name of Jesus. Amen.

After this, just consider this a call made to Jesus and say, "Please help my brothers [call the names written].'

Judas or Thaddaeus

Founder:
Jehovah Adonai Shaddai
Jesus Christ
Holy Spirit
12 Apostles

All the Holy Bible that worked through us your servants: Jorge, Veneranda, and Sarah Fecunda

If you want to subscribe, you can through this email address: fecundaj@hotmail.com.

London N. 3 April 2002

Freely you have received, freely give! (Matthew 10:8 NIV)

YES, WE BELIEVE MAGAZINE!

INTRODUCTION

Peter

This magazine will be based on twelve topics every month as we await the arrival of our Saviour, Jesus Christ. Walk with Jesus, our Saviour, as He lives through us with all His glory, sacrifices, riches, love, ministry, and prayer. God bless you as you take the time to see and read *Yes, We Believe Magazine!* It is unveiled to those who are being saved. It is written simply and humbly. All the glory to Jesus.

John

The Lord is not slow in keeping his promise, as some understand slowness. He is patient with you, not wanting anyone to perish, but everyone to come to repentance. This is the message we have from him and declare to you: God is light; in Him there is no darkness at all. If we claim to have fellowship with him yet walk in the darkness, we lie and do not live by truth. But if we walk in the light, as he is in the light, we have fellowship with one another, and the blood of Jesus, his Son, purifies us from all sin. If we claim to be without sin, we deceive ourselves and the truth is not in us. If we confess our sins, he is faithful and just and will forgive us our sins and purify us from all unrighteousness. If we claim we have not sinned, we make him out to be a liar and his word has no place in our lives.

2 Peter 3:9; 1 John 1:5–10

James

THIRD SPIRITUAL LETTER

The King will reply, "I tell you the truth, whatever you did for one of the least of these brothers of mine, you did for me".

Yours sons have fainted; they lie at the head of every street, like antelopoe caught in a net.

They are filled with the wrath of the lord and the rebuke of your God.

Therefore hear this, you afflicted one, made drunk, but not with wine. This is what your sovereign Lord says, your God, who defends his people: "see, I have taken out of your hand the cup that made you stagger; from that cup, the goblet of my wrath, you will never drink again".

"I will put it into the hands of your tormentors, who said to you fall prostrate that we may walk over you, and you made your back like the ground, like a street to be walked over".

For this is what the sovereign Lord says: "At first my people went down to Egypt to live; lately, Assyria has oppressed them. And now what do I have here?" declares the Lord. "For my people have been take away for nothing, and those who rule them mock" declares the Lord.

"And all day long my name is constantly blasphemed. Therfore my people will know my name; therefore in that day they will know that it is I who foretold it. Yes, it is I".

For this is what the Lord says: "You were sold for nothing, and without money you will be redeemed".

I tell you the tuth, anyone who gives you a cup of water in my name because you belong to Christ will certainly not lose his reward.

He who is kind to the poor lends to the Lord, and he will reward him for what he has done.

He who oppresses the poor shows contempt for their maker, but whoever is kind to the needy honours God.

God is not unjust; he will not forget your work and the love you have shown him as you have helped his people and continue to help them.

GLORY TO JESUS

Matthew 25:40; Isaiah 51:20-23; Isaiah 52:4, 5, 6, 3; Mark 9:41; Proverbs 19:17; Proverbs 14:31; Hebrews 6:10.

Andrew

OUR JOURNEY WITH JESUS
by V. Pallara Fecunda

Dear Sarah,

To continue last month's story . . .

Piu' forte e piu' salda e che nessuna chiave avrebbe potuto aprire quell'anello, una piccola chiave non poteva fare un lavoro cosi' grande. La sua incredulita', le costo' la divisione dal grande uccello. Il piccolo uccello soffri' tanto la mancanza del grande uccello, continuando a pregare il Creatore che li unisse di nuovo. Intanto il grande uccello stava pensando di riprendere il volo. Prima di farlo cerco' di sapere come il piccolo uccello stava e se voleva ancora seguirlo. Non potendo chiamare il piccolo uccello, per una promessa fatta, decise di comunicare con lei attraverso altri uccelli che non avevano pero', la sua stessa voce e il piccolo uccello ricevette un messaggio confuso e quando il grande uccello ando' al punto d'incontro non trovo' la sua piccola amica. Una voce dentro di se gli comunico': "Go, fly away", il, grande uccello si era pero'innamorato del piccolo (il quale invece si era innamorato del grande dal primo momento) e decise di aspettare un altro giorno. Il giorno dopo il piccolo uccello arrivo' con tutto il suo amore ma anche con tutta la sua confusione e debolezza tanto, che stava quasi per rinunciare al volo con il grande uccello perche' ancora aveva paura di utilizzare la chiave per aprire il piccolo anello ancora legato alla sua zampina. Quel giorno, Dio li mise in cuore di seguire il grande uccello e di utilizzare la piccola chiave di cui il grande uccello li aveva gia' tanto parlato, Gesu'. Quel giorno il piccolo uccello decise di utilizzare la chiave, apri' l'anello, lasciandolo

con amore perche' legato alla sua zampina fin dalla sua nascita, e
volo' via con il grande uccello.

    FINE

(Next month, there will be an English translation.)

Philip

NEWS FROM THE BIBLE

Do Not Worry

Therefore I tell you, do not worry about your life, what you will eat or drink; or about your body, what you will wear. Is not life more important than food, and the body more important than clothes? Look at the birds of the air; they do not sow or reap or store away in barns, and yet your heavenly Father feeds them. Are you not much more valuable than they? Who of you by worrying can add a single hour to his life? And why do you worry about clothes? See how the lilies of the field grow. They do not labour or spin. Yet I tell you that not even Solomon in all his splendour was dressed like one of these. If that is how God clothes the grass of the field, which is here today and tomorrow is thrown in the fire, will he not much more clothe you, O you of little faith? So do not worry, saying, 'What shall we eat?' or 'What shall we drink?' or 'What shall we wear?' For the pagans run after all these things, and your heavenly Father knows that you need them. But seek first his kingdom and his righteousness, and all these things will be given to you as well. Therefore do not worry about tomorrow, for tomorrow will worry about itself. Each day has enough trouble of its own.

Matthew 6:25–34 NIV

Judas or Thaddaeus

Prayer

People to pray for:

- David (Daud of the street)
- Mr Derrik Brown
- AnneMarie
- Christian brothers of TFC (Uxbridge Road)
- People of Israel
- Pastor Johnston and his congregation
- Universal Unity in Authority of Christianity in Faith

If you know how to pray this, then please do!

If you don't know and wish to pray, do this prayer:

'Jesus, I believe You are the Son of God who raised again and lived in the consciousness of man to teach and help us on our redemption and salvation.

Holy Spirit of Jesus, You are welcome in my temple [mind, body, and soul]. I will consider this done. Thank You, in the name of Jesus. Amen.

After this, just consider this a call made to Jesus and say, "Please help my brothers [call the names written].'

Thomas

EASTER FOR US BELIEVERS

As in this period where the believers remember Jesus Christ in Easter, I'm one who sees the good call of remembering our Saviour's appeal to man's consciousness by death on the cross to wash away our sins once and for always through His own blood and not that of animals, as this was done before Jesus Christ. However, I'm not one who sees the commercial show made out of it by, again, all who believe, for how long will we continue to deny the power of His blood and repetitively go through what is called the death and the resurrection of Christ? We believe He lives and that His followers are in this world, persecuted by the evil one—the spirit of the world—who do not believe that He is Christ. A city like London, as an example of this research done and posted in the local areas, quotes: 1 London, 14 faith, and 8 milion people. My point is this: that London has to cater for the peace of all these believers, by people who would know this, and find a way to make it work for all these people who has God in them. I always ask how much of God is in them. For by my teaching and doctrine of Christ, in the book of John 3:6, flesh gives birth to flesh, but the Spirit gives birth to the Spirit. In the book of Genesis 5:1–2 NIV, 'When God created man, he made him in the likeness of God. He created them male and female and blesed them. And when they were created, he called them man.' In Genesis 6:3, 'And then God said: My Spirit will not contend with man for ever.' In Genesis 6:5 NIV, 'Because, the Lord saw how great man's wickedness on the earth had become and that every inclination of the thought of his heart was only evil all the time.'

Through and through with all of God's love and consciousness, men of faith put through faith their works to share their perseverance and commitment according to God's design for them, by guidance of His Holy Spirit. We Christians have the story told through prophetic messages, and as we know the Bible to be a translation of this work of faith, we see what the Bible quotes. 'By imperfect man' that the translation done falls short of its goals, yet we are grateful to God for the extent to which He has enabled us to realise these goals and for the strength He has given us and our colleagues to complete our task Bible quote continue. We offer this version of the Bible to Him in whose name and for whose glory it has been made.

We pray that it will lead many into a better understanding of the Holy Scriptures and fuller knowledge of Jesus Christ, the incarnate Word of whom the Scriptures so faithfully testify. So if we are to reach unity in faith, it is to believe that all this has its working since the beginning of time and that people who wrote and recorded their work as faith in God all spoke of the same Saviour without living in the same time (epoch) or consulting one another and from many different walks of life. It's clear that when you believe, you'll see; for when you don't, the explanations are many. For belief in Jesus will open up your eyes to God's mysteries (miracles), and when you believe in the resurrection, you can't celebrate the death. It will mean going through all the things that were done before the death of Jesus Christ. For life is happening in you, for you are now no more your own but bought at a price, and the price is the blood shed, for God loves us, so He gave His only begotten Son for us who believe in Jesus to have eternal life. I encourage you, for now we know in part, then we shall know fully. Remember, I did say you've got to believe and have no doubt. If we truly believe, I'm having a challenge in understanding how we who call ourselves Christians can continue this joke of the commercial world, of what is also called the system. In Christmas, He's born, then we prepare for His Crucifixion and then His Resurrection and so on! It's a joke. We've got to take ourselves seriously and, yes, pray for more faith. In the Bible, 2 Corinthians 4:4 quotes, 'The God of this age blinded the mind of the unbelievers, so that they cannot see the light of the Gospel of the Glory of Christ, who is the image of God.' The image of God for believers in Jesus, Holy Spirit, and Jehovah Shaddai—the three-in-one. Yes, believers, let's repent and live with Jesus.

Bartholomew

TUTU, PRINCESS OF GOD

Tutu and her family arrived in Curaçao on 12 June 2001. They were happy to be in Curaçao (as I said the last time, God Almighty blessed them with a free air ticket to the island). Quickly the tribulations began and substituted their human joy, but Jesus was with them in all their tribulations so they could sing their joy in Christ every day and everywhere. The minister president of Curaçao allowed them to sing and praise God on the street. Their enemies increased after this meeting with the president. They lost their house, and for a week, they did not have a place to stay. In this week, Tutu was so strong. God gave her the strength. She was only five months in that period, thank God. She ate and slept every day at the same hour with or without a house, for three days in a hotel, and for four days on the street. After seven days, God, through an angel (his name is Mr Kleinmoedig), gave them a house. Thank You, Jesus. They suffered many tribulations in that week and many others after, but the love of Jesus was with them, so they won all the battles in His name.

(To be continued next month, in the name of Jesus.)

I hope with this story, the reader is not misled to confusion. Surely, one would ask, How come these people who live on the street have a story of an appointment with the minister president of the island? Why or how come they are undergoing so much tribulations? What are they doing? We proclaim the name of Jesus by living it through faith. This is enough to have miracles and tribulations all in the same day.

Tribulations are given by those who say they are Christians, but their hearts are far from the love of Christ Jesus, not accepting this family just because they have a different life. The miracle is manifested by the abundant love of God and mercy through mankind. Remember Genesis 1:27, 'We are made in his likeness.' God will never leave those who proclaim His holy name.

Matthew

MY TRUTH ABOUT MY CHRISTIAN LIFE
by V. Pallara Fecunda

This month I will pose a question to the readers. I asked myself the same question. Why do every church or every organisation (because there are many different denominations under the name Christian) think that they are the right place for the salvation of the souls? We do not appertain to any organisation. We are Christians, and we can congregate with all Christian believers. We have been in many different churches here in London as well as in many other countries like Italy, Germany, Holland, France, Spain, Portugal, Israel, USA, and Curaçao (Netherland Antilles); and I can say that in every place we have been, the Christian brothers cannot understand why we are only Christians. Often they did not accept us because we are not under their denomination. It's not enough to be Christian? It's not enough to follow Jesus? Do we really need a denomination? I never read in the Bible one of the many denominations that we have now; I read only about the Christian faith. In Romans 10:13, it is written, 'Everyone who calls on the name of the Lord will be saved.' And in Mark 9:38–40 NIV, '"Teacher, we saw a man driving out demons in your name and we told him to stop, because he was not one of us." "Do not stop him," Jesus said. "No one who does a miracle in my name can in the next moment say anything bad about me, for whoever is not against us is for us."'

Jesus did not say to His disciples, 'Well done, this man must follow us.' So why?

James

THE TABERNACLE

> Consider it pure joy, my brothers whenever you face
> trials of many kinds, because you know that the testing
> of your Faith develops perseverance. Perseverance must
> finish its work so that you may be mature and complete,
> not lacking anything. (James 1:2–4 NIV)

This is how we are going to give testimony to what happened on the first of March, the day of the Lord's tabernacle. Not knowing where it was to be held, we set out in faith to set up the Lord's tabernacle, which we believe by faith brings liberation, joy, love, and repentance all in the Spirit of our Lord Jesus, who does not need us, surely not. We are grateful to be part of what Jesus' doctrine, teachings and reading of the Bible, sharing through faith with all other believers have done, and are doing daily in our lives. So faithfully we have this ministry which is confirmed by the power of His Holy Spirit not by works but by the Spirit.

We ended up stopping at Trafalgar Square, where I stop in faith when I'm not sure I will stop and find out, for I will start. Readers, I started with a prayer; after the prayer, I set up the amplifier and guitar. With my wife, with her tambourine, and Sarah, our daughter, looking at us, I began to praise God in the presence of people, with the simple understanding of Genesis 1:27 NIV, 'And so God created the man in his own image, in the image of God he created him, male and female he created them.' I always ask, how much of God? As I was praising, he approached, yes, God, for the security guard also has God in him. Yes, we all are made in His likeness. So he said, 'I'm sorry, you cannot continue. I'm going to ask you to leave.' I responded, 'Hallelujah, I have a permit.' He said, 'Let's see it.' So when he saw what I had with me, he said, 'No this is for anywhere else, except here.' We discussed the matter for a few minutes, where I believe to have seen where his heart was. So yes, he said all the nice things such as anywhere else, he would have loved to listen to our songs.

We were asked to stop for this was his orders, and quote playing there we should have as well as he, a letter saying that we are to perform there on that date. Because of our conduct of peace, he asked which faith and god we're praising, and we shook hands. At that same time, I said God Almighty in the name of Jesus. Obviously, he was not of the same faith, but one thing he did agree in was the sentence 'We are created in the image of God.' Glory to the Lord. We moved on, and we glorified the name of Jesus a bit more after that. We changed to another place. Before stopping, we saw written on the brick wall was Lord, so I thought, *Hallelujah, our faith lives on.* So we stopped and set up there. We sang three songs and was threatened twice with death because of glorifying Jesus in that area. Okay, the area is one that needs liberation of chains of sexual immorality and a spirit that clearly is not pro-Christ but anti. Matthew 28:10, 19–20; Mark 13:10, 13. Readers, we have proclaimed Christ Jesus at Trafalgar Square, Charing Cross Road, and Newport. Glory to Jesus! Yes!

Matthias

AS WE CONTINUE TO TRAVEL IN FAITH
by J. Fecunda

On the twenty-fourth of March, there were again great testimonies. We sang in St Albans. This was great for praising God outside as it always has a special effect on us and those who come closer to us by faith, those in our faith rim of 0 to 12.000 km. I've done this close to the Roman Wall, which is something touristic. After praising—I was playing with Sarah, my daughter, for Mama Veneranda (Vera) just went to the toilet—to my surprise, I read what was written there which, if ever you are to go there, reader, you will see this notice engraved in the ground: Psalm 104:24. I believe from translation biblical King James Version. I took this as a personal message for me after praising. Thank You, Lord.

Simon

OPINION ON THIS QUESTION

What do you think about the abuse of the animals that are experimented on? I believe this question is answered sincerely, with nothing that we have for use or to master, should not be abused! And I think you would like me to say more about this and maybe share some insights from the Scriptures. Obviously, we are talking of the questions that believers would ask, agreeing to the faith we have in God Jehovah, the Scriptures, and the glory of our Saviour. In Genesis 1:28, it is written, 'Rule over fish, birds and every living creature that moves on the ground', referring to man to not abuse animals.

I believe next time, your question could be more specific about the word *abuse*, for there are many points of views. You'll probably like this written by King David's son in the Holy Bible, Ecclesiastes 3:18–19 NIV, 'I also thought, as for men, God tests them so that they may see that they are like the animals, Man's fate is like that of the animals; the same fate awaits them both: As one dies, so dies the other. All have the same breath; man has no advantage over the animal. Everything is meaningless.' About experiments on animals, I'll say we have our faith and know that there are other forces— conscience, powers, rulers, science—all of which when my opinion or your question is answered, we only have a comforting thought when we believe that God Almighty, creator of this universe, will judge it all, so don't worry. Remember, out of ±5 or 6 billion people, here is where you can make a difference—in faith and belief. Jesus was abused and killed for our sins. Invite Him in, and you'll understand everything better. Ecclesiastes 7:18 NIV states, 'The man who fears God will avoid all extremes.' Jorge Fecunda

I (Veneranda) agree with the answer of my husband, and I want to also say thanks to the people who are working to stop the abuse of animals because everyone of us has a different task, and the Bible says in Matthew 5:9 NIV, 'Blessed are the peacemakers, for they will be called sons of God.'

Founder:
Jehovah Adonai Shaddai
Jesus Christ
Holy Spirit
12 Apostoles

All the Holy Bible that worked through us your servants: Jorge, Veneranda, and Sarah Fecunda

London N. 4 May 2002

Freely you have received, freely give! (Matthew 10:8 NIV)

YES, WE BELIEVE MAGAZINE!

INTRODUCTION

Peter

This magazine will be based on twelve topics every month as we await the arrival of our Saviour, Jesus Christ. Walk with Jesus, our Saviour, as He lives through us with all His glory, sacrifices, riches, love, ministry, and prayer. God bless you as you take the time to see and read *Yes, We Believe Magazine!* It is unveiled to those who are being saved. It is written simply and humbly. All the glory to Jesus.

John

FOURTH SPIRITUAL LETTER

It is right for me to feel this way about all of you, since I have you in my hearth; for whether I'm in chains or defending and confirming the Gospel, all of you share in God's grace with me.

So that you may be able to discern what is best and may be pure and blameless until the day of Christ, filled with the fruit of righteousness that comes through Jesus Christ, to the glory and praise of God. And the Lord God said: "The man has now become like one of us, knowing good and evil. He must not be allowed to reach out his hand and take also from the tree of life and eat, and live for ever."

Being confident of this that he who began a good work in you will carry it on to completion until the day of Christ Jesus. GLORY TO JESUS

Philippians 1: 7, 10, 11; Genesis 3: 22; Philippians 1:6

James

PRAYER

People to pray for:

- Unity in Christianity
- Bob Gushue and family (Canada)
- Lucinda and daughters (Holland)
- Curtis and family (USA)
- Francesco Maggi, happy birthday, may God bless you! (Italy)
- Maggi Angelo as king of his palace (Italy)
- Benjamin (New Zealand)
- De Bonis Incoronata and her family (Italy)
- Beatrice, her husband, and family (Italy)
- John and Barbara (London)
- The landlord, the manager, and the staff of Royal Guest House Hotel (London)
- The people of Curaçao (Netherland Antilles)
- The United Kingdom

If you know how to pray this, then please do!

If you don't know and wish to pray, do this prayer:

'Jesus, I believe You are the Son of God who raised again and lived in the consciousness of man to teach and help us on our redemtion and salvation.

Holy Spirit of Jesus, You are welcome in my temple [mind, body, and soul]. I will consider this done. Thank You, in the name of Jesus. Amen.

After this, just consider this a call made to Jesus and say, "Please help my brothers [call the names written].'

If you want to subscribe, you can through this email address: fecundaj@hotmail.com.

Matthias

NEWS FROM THE BIBLE

God's Faithfulness

[1]What advantage, then, is there in being a Jew, or what value is there in circumcision? [2]Much in every way! First of all, they have been entrusted with the very words of God.

[3]What if some did not have faith? Will their lack of faith nullify God's faithfulness? [4]Not at all! Let God be true, and every man a liar. As it is written:

'So that you may be proved right
    when you speak
    and prevail when you judge.'[a]

[5]But if our unrighteousness brings out God's righteousness more clearly, what shall we say? That God is unjust in bringing his wrath on us? (I am using a human argument.) [6]Certainly not! If that were so, how could God judge the world? [7]Someone might argue, 'If my falsehood enhances God's truthfulness and so increases his glory, why am I still condemned as a sinner?' [8]Why not say——as we are being slanderously reported as saying and as some claim that we say——'Let us do evil that good may result?' Their condemnation is deserved.

No One Is Righteous

⁹What shall we conclude then? Are we any better?ᵇ Not at all! We have already made the charge that Jews and Gentiles alike are all under sin. ¹⁰As it is written:

> 'There is no-one righteous, not
>   even one:
> ¹¹ there is no-one who understands,
>   no-one who seeks God.
> ¹²All have turned away,
>   they have together become
>   worthless;
> there is no-one who does good,
>   not even one.'ᶜ
> ¹³'Their throats are open graves;
>   their tongues practise deceit.'ᵈ
>   'The poison of vipers is on their
>   lips.'ᵉ
> ¹⁴ 'Their mouths are full of cursing
>   and bitterness.'ᶠ
> ¹⁵'Their feet are swift to shed blood;
> ¹⁶ ruin and misery mark their ways,
> ¹⁷and the way of peace they do not know.'ᵍ
> ¹⁸ 'There is no fear of God before
>   their eyes,'ʰ

¹⁹Now we know that whatever the law says, it says to those who are under the law, so that every mouth may be silenced and the whole world held accountable to God. ²⁰Therefore no-one will be declared righteous in his sight by observing the law; rather, through the law we become conscious of sin.

Righteousness through Faith

[21]But now a righteousness from God, apart from law, has been made known, to which the Law and the Prophets testify. [22]This righteousness from God comes through faith in Jesus Christ to all who believe. There is no difference, [23]for all have sinned and fall short of the glory of God, [24]and are justified freely by his grace through the redemption that came by Christ Jesus. [25]God presented him as a sacrifice of atonement,[i] through faith in his blood. He did this to demonstrate his justice, because in his forbearance he had left the sins committed beforehand unpunished[26]––he did it to demonstrate his justice at the present time, so as to be just and the one who justifies those who have faith in Jesus.

[27]Where, then, is boasting? It is excluded. On what principle? On that of observing the law? No, but on that of faith. [28]For we maintain that a man is justified by faith apart from observing the law. [29]Is God the God of Jews only? Is he not the God of Gentiles too? Yes, of Gentiles too, [30]since there is only one God, who will justify the circumcised by faith and the uncircumcised through that same faith. [31]Do we, then, nullify the law by this faith? Not at all! Rather, we uphold the law.

Romans 3 NIV

Judas or Thaddaeus

OPINION ON THIS QUESTION
by J. Fecunda

What is your purpose with this A3 you call a magazine?

Well, you know how much is shared in this world, good and bad things, killing and life-giving things right! We have faith, that's it. Without action, this is dead, so in this surpassing world, we are filled with the living Spirit of Christ Jesus. Have faith that this A3, as you know, will continue to unfold the encouragement and works and testimonies of faith by people of faith who believes in the Resurrection of our Lord and Saviour!

PS. The Holy Bible says, 'I pray that you may be active in sharing your Faith, so that you will have a full understanding of every good thing we have in Christ' (Philemon 1:6).

Philip

If you want to share your testimony about Unity in Christianity, you can at fecundaj@hotmail.com.

UNITY IN CHRISTIANITY

if you love one another.' Romans 13:8–10 NIV states, 'Let no debt remain outstanding, except the continuing debt to love one another, for he who loves his fellow-man has fulfiled the law.' The commandments 'Do not commit adultery', 'Do not murder', 'Do not steal', 'Do not covet', and whatever other commandment there may be are summed up in this one rule—love your neighbour as yourself. Love does no harm to its neighbour. Therefore, love is the fulfilment of the law. 1 John 3:19–20 NIV states, 'This then is how we know that we belong to the truth, and how we set our hearts at rest in his presence whenever our hearts condemn us. For God is greater than our hearts, and he knows everything.' John 15:17 NIV says, 'This is my command: Love each other.' 1 John 3:21–24 NIV states, 'Dear friends, if our hearts do not condemn us, we have confidence before God and receive from him anything we ask, because we obey his commands and do what pleases him. And this is his command: to believe in the name of his Son, Jesus Christ, and to love one another as he commanded us. Those who obey his commands live in him, and he in them. And this is how we know that he lives in us: We know it by the Spirit he gave us.'

By faith, you will understand. Just believe, says Jesus! The story continues.

After staying there for approximately one month and one week, we left with our faith of the ministry the Lord gave us: to be obedient to the Spirit of the Lord Almighty, better known as the Holy Spirit. We left Pastor Paul and his congregation and went to Amsterdam, Italy, and back to England. And then again after this, we were sent to address the call of the Lord in the name of

Jesus in the Caribean. The Lord is awesome; we are grateful to be His friends and servants. All these confessions and testimonial stories are to tell you that today, the pastor saw again how great is his and our God in the name of Jesus, for I always said he's a man of God Almighty. For often these men of God get caught by the evil in them—*ego* and *denomination*—and forget the true work of God, which is humble and gratifying and does not seek glory, for all the glory is to Jesus, who is the mediator of God Almighty Jehovah, and man is made in His likeness.

In last month's edition of *Yes, We Believe Magazine*, I prayed for Unity in Authority in Christianity, for I truly believe in what the word of the Bible said that we will all reach unity in faith in the Son of God, Christ Jesus. Oh, and in this race, as Apostle Paul says or puts it, Jesus said, 'I will go and prepare a place especially for you!' So why this *segregation*? Making Jesus into this God of. We have it, and our denomination is the one making the rules and forgetting what the Bible says in the book of 2 John 1:6–9 NIV, 'And this is love that we walk in obedience to his commands. As you have heard from the beginning, his command is that you walk in love. Many deceivers, who do not acknowledge Jesus Christ as coming in the flesh have gone out into the world. Any such person is the deceiver and the antichrist. Watch out that you do not lose what you have worked for, but that you may be rewarded fully. Anyone who runs ahead and does not continue in the teaching of Christ does not have God; whoever continues in the teaching has both the Father and the Son.'

My point here is, the Spirit guides you to understand that faith without action is dead and reaching unity in faith is to start breaking down the wall of segregation of Christ in faith, bringing about the love and submission of the *ego*, and bringing out the godly or let your light shine. Yes, God bless Pastor Paul, for he believed and saw God's blessing in his congregation today. Readers, this is my testimony. Full Gospel Church in Brixton received faith with the action of the pastor. We sang and glorified by praising, and the miracle of the Holy Spirit has filled the church and everyone there that Sunday, 14/04/2002. Glory to Jesus! If you want to encourage them, you can at Brixton Full Gospel Church. It may or may not be in our lifetime when Jesus will appear with all His glory, but unity in faith was answered in our prayer by our testimony. Family Fecunda: Jorge, Veneranda, and Sarah. Amen. Thank You, Jesus.

James

UNITY IN CHRISTIANITY
by J. Fecunda

Glory to Jesus!

To the ones we reached with this humble writing of our faith experiences, may the miracle of this story touch you as you read this and understand our faith in Christianity by faith. We were invited to sing for a Christian congregation that blessed us once before. By faith, we met them, and yes, I'll emphasise this. We were in Brixton on a Saturday because I felt that I had to go to Brixton, not knowing the purpose. I was obedient to the voice that I encourage others to develop according to what you feed it. This grows stronger, and I call this the voice of God in me. If I forgot to tell you, I feed on the Word of God written out of sixty-six books over a period of ±1,500 years, culminating approximately 100 years after Christ's death and resurrection. So yes, as I was saying, I've learnt to be obedient to the voice of God in me.

We went to Brixton, and when we were to return to Hammersmith, my wife saw a manifestation which called her attention and was taken by this, for we glorify the Lord on the street. I believe this was the first time she saw a manifestation like this that touched her—a group of Koreans praising God in the name of Jesus. We approached and, yes, was also approached by God. I believe I keep reminding the readers we are all made in God's likeness. I also say how much of God, because there is also evil. Yes, God asked us how we are, and we said to God, 'Good, thanks.' We also praised Jesus, so the pastor said, 'Yes! How great and we fellowship and discerned each other.' Readers, I know you are saying how come one moment I say God and then I'm discerning? Yes, we also know that the evil knows the Bible, and he is known to present himself as an angel of light. So we need to discern, and to do this, we need to know the Spirit of Jesus. The evil cannot have this. Once having the Spirit of Jesus, it/he is a new creation under the New Covenant, which is bought by the blood. 'Hallelujah.' So this is why we need to discern, for there are many false prophets out there.

So long story short, we accepted God's invitation through Pastor Paul and visited on a Sunday. This brought blessing by tribulations and made us stronger, for we persevered in what God told us by prophetic messages and laying of hand and walks with Jesus before meeting the pastor. God bless us. We would like to talk about this right now as the story continued today. We stayed at this house, a vicarage, called by the pastor a hospital for the spirit. This was because in that same period, I lost my job, which I believe God's wonders and mysteries knew why. However, Pastor Paul, after fellowship, offered us a caravan in the yard. My wife, having Sarah, said, 'We are really going to take this?' I said, 'We'll pray and have faith that God will show the way.' Okay! She . . . okay! Yes, this was God's will for us after prayer. We stayed there, and in the same week, I started to work again. Then we were offered a room in the house because of Sarah, our daughter. God blessed us like this through the two missionary brothers now in Korea. They had the room and said, 'We'll let them have it.' Praise Jesus. Thank You, God.

I stayed there, and the fellowship grew strong and showed that *we are a nation under the blood and the anointing of the Lord Jesus without a denomination.* We will and can congregate in the name of Jesus. After this, obviously there are spiritual battles to overcome, but in faith, we follow the Lord's command as He said He will give two new commands in the book of Mark 12:28–31 NIV: 'One of the teachers of the law came and heard them debating. Noticing that Jesus had given them a good answer, he asked him, of all the commandments which is the most important? The most important one answered Jesus is this: Hear, O Israel, the Lord our God, the Lord is one. Love the Lord your God with all your heart and with all your soul and with all your mind and with all your strength.

The second is this: Love your neighbour as yourself. There is no commandment greater than these.'

So my point is, yes, there are spiritual battles to overcome, but it's only spiritual, not against flesh, like our forefathers understood with the sword. For if you understood this single two commandments Jesus said, you are not far from the kingdom. Readers, here are some more of this same spiritual food for you: If you like, read John 13:34–35 NIV: 'A new command I give you: Love one another. As I have loved you, so you must love one another. By this all men will know that you are my disciples,

Matthew

OUR JOURNEY WITH JESUS
by V. Pallara Fecunda

Dear Sarah,

This time, finally I'll make a short English translation of the bird's story. This story speaks of a meeting between two birds—the big one, J., and smaller one, V.

J. is a bird big and strong. He travelled a lot. His life is to praise his Creator, who gave him a wonderful voice. In one of his travels, he met V., the small bird. When V. saw J. for the first time, she liked his strength, his beauty, and his faith. She said to him, 'Big bird, I cannot fly, but I believe that with you, I will be able to fly.' The big bird knew very well the problem of the little one. She could not fly because she had on one of her little leg a little ring with a chain; this ring linked her to the earth. She never saw this ring before. J. showed her the problem, and she was sad. She said, 'What can I do? With this ring, I cannot fly. I cannot follow you, and I love you.'

J. answered, 'Yes, you can. I have the key!'

'The key?' she said. 'It's impossible.' V. started to become nervous, and she did not have the strength to open the ring. The situation of the ring brought her far from J. The two birds were sad, and God heard their prayers. The big bird came back, and little one was so happy, but she still had the little ring on her leg.

J. said to her, 'I will fly away. Do you want to come with me?'

She said, 'Oh, please don't go away. You know I cannot fly because of the ring that I have. Please wait for me!' But God Almighty knew her heart, so He gave her the strength to use the key to open up the ring. The key is Jesus. Finally, V. was free. She left the ring on the earth, and she flew away with J., the big bird, to follow Jesus. From their love, God blessed them, and V. gave birth to a little bird. Bird S. is a beautiful gift from God Almighty.

The End

Andrew

For Christ did not send me to baptise, but to preach the gospel, not with words of human wisdom, lest the cross of Christ be emptied of its power. For the message of the cross is foolishness to those who are perishing, but to us who are being saved it is the power of God. For it is written: 'I will destroy the wisdom of the wise; the intelligence of the intelligent I will frustrate.' Where is the wise man? Where is the scholar? Where is the philosopher of this age? Has not God made foolish the wisdom of the world? For since in the wisdom of God the world through its wisdom did not know him, God was pleased through the foolishness of what was preached to save those who believe. Jews demand miraculous signs and Greeks look for wisdom, but we preach Christ crucified: a stumbling block to Jews and foolishness to Gentiles, but to those whom God has called, both Jews and Greeks, Christ the power of God and the wisdom of God. For the foolishness of God is wiser than man's wisdom, and the weakness of God is stronger than man's strength. Brothers, think of what you were when you were called. Not many of you were wise by human standards; not many were influential; not many were of noble birth. But God chose the foolish things of the world to shame the wise; God chose the weak things of the world to shame the strong. He chose the lowly things of this world and the despised things, and the things that are not, to nullify the things that are, so that no one may boast before him. It is because of him that you are in Christ Jesus, who has become for us wisdom from God that is, our righteousness, holiness and redemption. Therefore, as it is written: 'Let him who boasts boast in the Lord.'

1 Corinthians 1:17–31 NIV

Bartholomew

THE TABERNACLE
by V. Pallara Fecunda

In April we made the tabernacle of the Lord in Godolphin Park. If you have read already *Yes, We Believe Magazine*, you know that every first of the month, we make the tabernacle of the Lord by faith. Our faith is that in every place we are praising and glorifying God in the name of Jesus, there will be healing, liberation, and joy, all in the Spirit and through the power of the Holy Spirit. As I said in *Yes, We Believe Magazine* on March, *faith is being sure of what we hope for and certain of what we do not see.* This time, I saw what I believe. When we arrived at the park, I saw two women with their children, but one of them took more my attention. Why? She was playing with her child but not with joy (this is my opinion of course). When my husband, Jorge, started to praise, I was thinking about this woman, and I prayed to God for her. To praise God is so beautiful and joyful, and the presence of the Holy Spirit makes the people so free, without inhibition. Sarah, our daughter, enjoyed herself in the park. She danced, walked, and played; and I did the same. I also shared with her my tambourine. My husband was praising and praying with the guide of the Holy Spirit all the time. In the middle of the praise, I saw the woman with her child clap their hands and dance; they also were happy. When we finished, she passed and said, 'Thank you for your music.' I gave her a CD and a *Yes, We Believe Magazine.* She was full of joy. God bless her and her child. Again my testimony is about the power of the Holy Spirit, because only the Spirit of Christ Jesus can make the people joyful and drunk without drinking wine. Acts 2:1–13. Glory to Jesus!

Simon

TUTU, PRINCESS OF GOD

Tutu's family left Curaçao on 2 October 2001. They went to Miami, where a Christian family gave them the hospitality in their property, in a tent, not knowing that that night in Miami, there was gale and strong rain. At midnight, the father was busy doing everything possible for the water that entered the tent, ±2 cm on the inside edge of the tent. With prayer and wisdom, the father kept them all in the middle of the tent, dry. Thank You, Jesus.

Tutu suffered many things. She was only eight months old, and she saw her father give all his attention to another child, the daughter of the other family. She suffered in silence, but her mother saw her suffering. The father loved her, but in his spiritual work for God, he helps other people. And often, people want more and more of this attention when they see that the attention comes from a man of God. Often I saw that human beings become hungry of this clean love because it's the love of Jesus. Tutu was quiet and patience all the time, and the mother saw all these things. For Tutu's patience and love, the father learned many things from that situation. In fact, now with his growth, he can give to Tutu and her mother and also to others, because God gives him. The whole family learned from this situation that sometimes when we want to do the work for God and help and save souls, we forget the people who are near us, like our husbands, wives, and children. Thank You, Jesus, for the wisdom and for our love in Christ Jesus that is given to all abundantly. Until next month when we continue the true story of Tutu, princess of God.

Founder:
Jehovah Adonai Shaddai
Jesus Christ

Holy Spirit
12 Apostoles

All the Holy Bible that worked through us your servants: Jorge,
Veneranda, and Sarah Fecunda

London N. 5 June 2002

Freely you have received, freely give! (Matthew 10:8 NIV)

YES, WE BELIEVE MAGAZINE

INTRODUCTION

John

This magazine will be based on twelve topics every month as we await the arrival of our Saviour, Jesus Christ. Walk with Jesus, our Saviour, as He lives through us with all His glory, sacrifices, riches, love, ministry, and prayer. God bless you as you take the time to see and read *Yes, We Believe Magazine!* It is unveiled to those who are being saved. It is written simply and humbly. All the glory to Jesus.

Judas or Thaddaeus

The festival was nearly half over when Jesus went to the Temple and began teaching. The Jewish authorities were greatly surprised and said, 'How does this man know so much when he has never had any training?' Jesus answered, 'What I teach is not my own teaching, but it comes from God, who sent me. Whoever is willing to do what God wants will know whether what I teach comes from God or whether I speak on my own authority. A person who speaks on his own authority is trying to gain glory for himself. But he who wants glory for the one who sent him is honest, and there is nothing false in him.

John 7:14–18 GNT

Founder:
Jehovah Adonao Shaddai
Jesus Christ
Holy Spirit
12 Apostles

All the Holy Bible that worked through us your servants: Jorge, Veneranda, and Sarah Fecunda

If you want to subscribe, you can at fecundaj@hotmail.com.

Philip

THE STORY OF THE FIRST AND SECOND CASSETTE
by J. Fecunda

With our faith of Christianity without a denomination or an organisation backing us or funding us, we stand by the grace of the Lord Jesus through the power of grace. This is *our faith*. Five thousand plus cassettes of our previous recording done in 1999 in Curaçao (Netherland Antilles) have been shared, like I have already said, to some people as gifts while others in exchange for money, depending on where we were in the world. Angelo Maggi, a Christian brother, blessed us with a production of 3,000 CDs of which he is also doing the distribution and blessing people of faith in Italy. He was on a visit in London and brought us 125 CDs of which he said, 'A present for you from us the Maggi family.' By this story, I hope to thank them and encourage their Christian Heart. May they always have to give in the name of Jesus Christ, who said, 'It's more blessed to give than to receive' (Acts 20:35). We have shared these CDs with love ones for it's the work of faith that we do! And when God works through us by having others to support, like Angelo Maggi did, without me asking. Hallelujah! After all, I'm singing to encourage faith, for faith has its measures as the Lord said, according to the level of faith that you have been given. We see this as an area where we can encourage, for we have been given substantial. And thank God for we are in service of the Lord Christ Jesus. If you like a copy, I'm to say, his email address is obrigadoj@hotmail.com. Obviously, I don't know his arrangements, and please understand that he speaks Italian and is learning English, so be patient. However, if you just want a cassette of our first and second recording, I hope with faith to have for you, reader, a double-cassette pack in the near future. Everything is in prayer, and when you live with consciousness and seek first His kingdom, the Lord will give the things you ask for in the name of Jesus. Oh, if you want to intercede for us with your prayer, thank you, and may God bless you and us. Amen.

Bartholomew

THE TABERNACLE

The first of May, we set up the tabernacle of the Lord in Piccadilly Circus, not knowing that day was Mayday. We took the bus from Hammersmith Station, and quite a few stops before Piccadilly, the bus stopped. The area was full of police agents. After stepping out, the Spirit (God's Spirit) made us aware that there was something going on. Only we did not know, and we did not want to ask. So we walked a little bit to understand if that was the right place for our tabernacle as my husband is always guided by the Holy Spirit for the exact place to praise, because this was the day of the tabernacle for us. And as you know, with our faith, we believe this brings joy, liberation, and peace. We stopped in front of Piccadilly Circus, and we felt the tension in the area when we started to praise. We understood that there was a need for peace. Many people stopped to understand what we were doing. Simply with love, we were glorifying the holy name of Jesus.

After 5 songs, we saw the arrival of the anarchic demonstration, so we stopped because of our peace. Our God is a god of peace, and we do not want to disturb others in their belief. Glory to Jesus. That day, our voice was heard glorifying the name of Jesus. We continued our walk of faith. For a few minutes, I saw my past in those people, and I said, 'Thank You, Jesus, for the life of truth I live now with You.' We left Piccadilly and went to St James Park, where we drunk a cup of hot chocolate, and we continued with our tabernacle, praising the Lord.

We are grateful for the things the Lord allows us to see through this faith of glorifying His holy name. Sarah danced and played her maracas, ± 20 people were in our surrounding, and with the peace given by the Spirit, some were laying in the grass, some drinking, some kissing and talking, while others were just looking. Thank God, in the wonderful name of Jesus!

Simon

TUTU PRINCESS OF GOD

Tutu is now almost sixteen months old. As I said in the first issue of *Yes, We Believe Magazine*, she has been already in different countries, like Italy, Holland, Curaçao (Netherland Antilles), and USA. She was born in London. She is always with her father and mother when they pray or glorify Jesus on the street or in a congregation. When they praise God, she plays her maracas, and she likes to pray too. Sometimes when she is hungry, it's so hard to wait for Abba (daddy) to close the prayer. Tutu, princess of God, is a real gift of God to her parents. They know also that it's important to ask wisdom from God to parent a child. You don't know, maybe one day, if God wants, you will meet Tutu on the street with her parents and her maracas to praise God Almighty in the name of Jesus, as the Psalm 117 GNT says, 'Praise the Lord, all nations! Praise him, all peoples! His love for us is strong and his faithfulness is eternal. Praise the Lord!'

(Until next month when we continue the true story of Tutu, princess of God.)

Grida nel deserto

Servant to the Lord
Jorge M. Fecunda

Peter

Fifth Spiritual Letter

Some men brought to him a paralytic, layng on a mat. When Jesus saw their faith, he said to the paralytic, "Take hearth, son; your sins are forgiven."

Jesus Christ is the same yesterday and today and for ever. As a result, he does not live the rest of his earthly life for evil human desires, but rather for the will of God.

And so Jesus also suffered outside the city gate to make the people holy through his own blood. Let us, then, go to him outside the camp, bearing the disgrace he bore.

And he died for all, that those who live should no longer live for themselves but for him who died for them and was raised again.

For here we do not have an enduring city; but we are looking for the city that is to come.

Keep on loving each other as brothers. Do not forget to entertain strangers, for by so doing some people have entertained angels without knowing it.

And do not forget to do good and to share with others, for with such sacrifices God is pleased.

Remember those in prison as if you were their fellow-prisoners, and those who are ill-treated as if you yourselves were suffering.

Marriage should be honoured by all, and the marriage bed kept pure, for God will judge the adulterer and all the sexually immoral.

Keep your lives free from the love of money and be content with what you have, because God has said, "Never will I leave you; never I will forsake you."

So we say with confidence, "The Lord is my helper; I will not be afraid. What can man do to me?

Don't you know that when you offer yourselves to someone to obey him as slaves, you are slaves to the one whom you obey, whether you are slaves to sin, wich leads to death, or to obedience, wich leads to righteousness?

Do not be carried away by all kinds of strange teachings. It is good for our hearts to be strengthened by grace, not by cerimonial foods, wich are of no value to those who eat them.

Remember your leaders, who spoke the word of God to you. Consider the outcome of their way of life and imitate their faith.

Obey your leaders and submit to their authority. They keep watch over you as men who must give an account. Obey them so that their work will be a joy, not a burden, for that would be of no advantage to you.

I have been crucified with Christ and I no longer live, but Christ lives in me. The life I live in the body, I live by faith in the Son of God, who loved me and gave himself for me.

In the same way, count yourselves dead to sin but alive to God in Christ Jesus. Therefore do not let sin reign in your mortal body so that you obey its evil desires. Do not offer the parts of your body to sin, as instruments of wickedness, but rather offer yourselves to God, as those who have been brought from death to life; and offer the parts of your body to him as instuments of righteousness.

Because our gospel came to you not simply with words, but also with power, with the Holy Spirit and with deep conviction. You know how we lived among you for your sake.

For sin shall not be your master, because you are not under law, but under grace.

Finally, be strong in the Lord and in his mighty power.

Therefore put on the full armour of God, so that when the day of evil comes, you may be able to stand your ground, and after you have done everything, to stand. Stand firm then, with the belt of truth buckled round your waist, with the breastplate of righteousness in place, and with your feet fitted with the readiness that comes from the gospel of peace. In addition to all this, take up the shield of faith, with which you can extinguish all the flaming arrows of the evil one. Take the helmet of salvation and the sword of the Spirit, which is the word of God. And pray in the Spirit on all occasions with all kinds of prayers and requests.

May the God of peace, who trough the blood of eternal covenant brought back from the dead our Lord Jesus, that great Shepherd of the sheep, equip you with everything good for doing his will, and may he work in us what is pleasing to him, through Jesus Christ, to whom be glory for ever and ever. Amen

Glory to Jesus

Matthew 9: 2; Hebrews 13:8; 1 Peter 4:2; Hebrews 13: 12, 13; 2 Corinthians 5: 15; Hebrews 13: 14, 1, 2, 16, 3-6; Romans 6: 16; Hebrews 13: 9, 7, 17; Galatians 2: 4; Hebrews 13: 18; Galatians 2: 20; Romans 6: 11, 13; 1 Thessalonians 1: 5; Romans 6: 14; Ephesians 6: 10, 13-18; Hebrews 13: 20, 21.

Andrew

MY TRUTH ABOUT MY CHRISTIAN LIFE
by J. Fecunda

First of all, I want to thank You, God, for my breath; and I'm confident about that neither life nor death will ever separate me from you, Jesus. Every so often, there are a lot of questions in every man's mind about God, and they conclude with 'You know for yourself, I'm guessing'. Well, yes, of course, there is a god up there!

Here is my truth about my Christian life. There is an ignorance to the person Jesus. When I talk about my truth of Christian life, for me it is to talk about Christ Jesus. This is the story told through generations of believers and, yes, also pulled and stretched by the commercial world. Not to forget religion, they played their part in this as well, and now you have simply (me) my faith and belief, telling you my truth! One thing I must say before I continue is, God Almighty, Jesus, and the Holy Spirit is personal and universal. This is part of the truth I must tell. Jesus is preached, and yet there is disagreement about who is saying what. This is not only now but all throughout the historical time. If you know of the ministry of Apostle Paul, he fought the not accepted of believers (Christians) apart from proclaiming Jesus to Jews and Greeks (Gentiles). I like this where he says in the book of Acts 20:23–24 NIV, 'I only know that in every city the Holy Spirit warns me that prison and hardships are facing me: however I consider my life worth nothing to me, if only I may finish the race and complete the task the Lord Jesus has given me, the task of testifying to the Gospel of God's grace.' This was a man who persecuted Christians until . . . I hope to interest you to read about this man in chapter 22 of the book of Acts in the Bible.

I'm showing this point to say that up until today, we segregate. All this was happening already, the so-called segregation of the body of Christ, for some preach a financial Christ and some a grace Christ. My truth is that this is possible for Jesus is personal, and after this conscious knowing of Jesus, there is the part of rebirth by Spirit and water, all under faith of any spiritual Christian overseer, i.e. pastor. Then you have got to walk the walk of faith in order to grow—yes, like a baby, we are then to grow by milk, care, love, and guidance. When this is done in faith, yes, you can grow with your Bible for the grace of the Holy Spirit will guide you for this. One will need to know the voice of the Holy Spirit for, yes, He will come in and take His place when you've invited Him in. Mr Fecunda, what are you saying? That one can grow just by faith and reading the Bible? I'm saying that *God is greater* than what human beings make out of the doctrine of Christ, their control, and lack of knowledge in keeping someone from knowing what God freely give to those who truly seek to know God's truth.

In the Bible, there are two quotes. I would like to share them with you.

> But what does it say? The word is near you; it is in your mouth and in your hearth, that is the word of faith we are proclaiming: That if you confess with your mouth, Jesus is Lord and believe in your hearth that God raised him from the dead you will be saved. For it is with your hearth that you believe and are justified, and it's with your mouth that you confess and are saved. As the Scriptures says, 'Anyone who trusts in him will never be put to shame.' (Romans 10:8–11 NIV)

> I know that after I leave, savage wolves will come in among you and will not spare the flock. Even from your own number men will arise and distort the truth in order to draw away disciples after them. So be on your guard! Remember that for three years I never stopped warning each of you night and day with tears. Now I commit you to God and to the word of his grace, which can build you up and give you an inheritance among all those who

are sanctified. I have not coveted anyone's silver or gold or clothing. You yourselves know that these hands of mine have supplied my own needs and the needs of my companions. (Acts 20:29–34 NIV)

Clearly, we can understand this man is our spiritual leader. His encouragement should unify us under the faith, belief, and blood of Christ Jesus. Okay, see if you can understand my points:

1. Confess and believe in Jesus.
2. Read your Bible; all stories are to show that God was always seeking repentance and obedience so He can pour out His love.
3. Seek righteousness in everything you do.
4. *Congregate*—this means speak to people (positively) who are *like-minded.* For example, if you speak to robbers and liars, you will eventually lie because it will rub off on you or become second nature to you. *This is why Christians should congregate.* So yes, the church is a building where people congregate, *but not only* the church, for *I strongly advice* that the first place to congregate is at home with *your partner (wife) and kids.*
5. Don't enslave yourselves to the worldly desires.
6. There is *no condemnation in Christ Jesus* if you are under His blood and the guidance of His Holy Spirit, which now you know how to attain (Romans 10:8–11).
7. Yes, when strength are put together, there is power, but also be aware of the *integrity of this unity for, first of all, Christianity is about love, not financial gain.* This is what Paul said. He worked for his necessities. Here this suppose to encourage men of God not to covet because they bring a gift given by the Lord free of charge to build His nation (people) in *unity of faith,* not financial gain. Remember the story in the book of Mark 10:17–25: 'His face fell after hearing what he must do.' It's clear that we need finance to trade in this world.'

I'm just sharing my truth to say pay attention, use it well as a *means to an end*, because you cannot take it with you. Even here, the Holy Spirit is capable to guide one and when you have a relationship with Him! (The Father, the Holy Spirit, and Jesus is three-in-one.) These things are my truths about my Christian life. They also tried to divide Christ by what a man must eat. Romans 14:22 NIV states, 'So whatever you believe about these things keep between yourself and God. Blessed is the man who does not condemn himself by what he approves.' If you want to know more about it, read all the verses in Romans 14. *Jesus is real!* I hope this cleared a bit of ignorance about Jesus *as a man*, now living in Spirit in the man who repents and asks him in. Oh, He said we will do more than He did. *He never spoke of money.* He said give God what belongs to God. On the coin in those days was the face of Caesar, so give Caesar what belongs to him. Isn't He just simple, awesome, almighty? It is also written in John 21:25 NIV, 'All the things he did, the world would not have room for the books that would be written.'

GOD BLESS YOU IN THE NAME OF JESUS, OUR SAVIOUR.

EVERY FIRST OF THE MONTH WE HOLD BY FAITH THE TABERNACLE TO SAY THANK YOU AND TO CALL THE PRESENCE OF THE LORD JESUS CHRIST. OUR FAITH IS THAT THIS BRINGS HEALINGS, JOY AND ALL THAT THE HOLY SPIRIT REVEALS TO THOSE OF FAITH.

James

OPINION ON THIS QUESTION
by V. Pallara Fecunda

Can you tell me your opinion about the anarchic life you knew and the life you live now? Yes, I was anarchic. I was born in a Catholic family. I knew Jesus, but not with the conscience I have now. In my faith, I wanted something more. What did I want? In that period, I did not know. I did not want to be a hypocrite and to say, 'I have peace with my faith.' Many times I said to my mother, 'If God wants, one day I will have a big *faith*.' I wanted to be near God, but I did not know how. I remember when I was sixteen years old, I have read the whole Bible. I prayed a lot, and I had a period of fasting.

When I started college, the situation became worse. In many books that I have read in that period, I discovered a lot of wrong the people have done in the name of Jesus. I became angry. 'How can the people of God make so much evil to other human being?' I asked myself. I have asked the same question to other people, even to my mother, and she said, 'Have faith. Don't look at what the priest does, but listen to what the priest says.' I did not accept her answer, and I became more and more angry. What happened? I started a personal battle against the church, the political system, but not against God or Jesus. I defined myself as anarchic-communist, and I met like-minded people with the same questions. At first I was happy with the answers I have gathered among my new friends. Later I saw also hypocrisy in that world—the rebels world! I myself was a hypocrite—in the first place with myself and after with other people. I remember we could speak for hours between beer and a glass of wine about issues like the peace in the world, the right reason of the communism, etc. But our talking was without actions, and often I woke up with a headache. I was so confused.

Once upon a time, I said to my sister that for me, Jesus was a big man, like Che Guevara. *I was so far from the truth*, and when I met my husband, Jorge, I asked him that same question: 'How can the people of God make so much evil to other human being?' He answered me with the Bible—Revelation 22:11–21. I liked his answer, and I have read these verses for one week. Finally, I started to see the simplicity and how humble Jesus is. If we think a little bit like this man, with Him being humble and without organisation, He said and did radical things in His peaceful way. He said, 'I am the bread of life, those who come to me will never be hungry, those who believe in me will never be thirsty. Now i told you that you have seen me but will not believe. Everyone whom my Father gives me will come to me, because I have come down from heaven to do not my own will but the will of him who sent me. And it is the will of him who sent me that I should not lose any of all those he has given me, but that I should raise them all to life on the last day. For what my Father wants is that all who see the Son and believe in him should have eternal life. And I will raise them to life on the last day' (John 6:35–40 GNT). He came more than 2,000 years ago, and we are still talking about Him. If you don't believe that He is the Son of God, look at what He had done and does, because Jesus still lives in everyone who believes in Him. We cannot say the same of anyone else, His name brings peace, liberation, and healing. If you call His name, you can see. If you call His presence in you—in your soul, body, and mind—you can see what will happen. Don't be afraid. You will be free.

Now I can say with joy that I am a Christian. Yes, I know of a lot of wrong done in Jesus' name, but I learnt also that I cannot judge. Only God can do this, and He will judge me for the evil and the good I have done and will also judge you, reader, and every human being, believer or not. So I stopped to look what others have done and do in His name, and I started to become conscious of what I can really do. Thank You, Lord, for that day and for my husband, because through him, you gave me knowledge that day.

Matthew

NEWS FROM THE BIBLE

But mark this: There will be terrible times in the last days. People will be lovers of themselves, lovers of money, boastful, proud, abusive, disobedient to their parents, ungrateful, unholy, without love, unforgiving, slanderous, without self-control, brutal, not lovers of the good, treacherous, rash, conceited, lovers of pleasure rather than lovers of God, having a form of godliness but denying its power. Have nothing to do with them. They are the kind who worm their way into homes and gain control over weak-willed women, who are loaded down with sins and are swayed by all kinds of evil desires, always learning but never able to acknowledge the truth. Just as Jannes and Jambres opposed Moses, so also these men oppose the truth, men of depraved minds, who, as far as the faith is concerned, are rejected. But they will not get very far because, as in the case of those men, their folly will be clear to everyone.

2 Timothy 3:1–9 NIV

LONDON

Happy news from London. Our CD made by faith in Curaçao was given for free to almost 125 people, and it's now sold in KCD, 142 Uxbridge Road, Shepherd's Bush Green, London, W12 8AA (tel. 020 8740 7500), for five pounds. The name of the CD is *Grida nel deserto* by Jorge M. Fecunda. For us, this is a big surprise and a big encouragement to see that the owner of the shop decided this price for our CD, a higher price than other CDs made by famous people. It's incredible. When God wants something, the power of the world can do nothing against His will. So if you want to buy this work of faith, you can at the above address for five pounds. All the glory to Jesus. The same CD was playing for one hour in a cafe in Goldhawk Road. Pacific.net. For us, this was so beautiful to listen to in a place that is not a Christian place. It's not a church; it's a simple cafe where the name of Jesus was glorified for one hour in a loud voice. We saw that it's possible to have praise songs in a cafe even when the name of Jesus is glorified *not offensive to no one*, when the purpose is clean and not wanting nothing! Glory to Jesus.

Matthias

CELEBRATION
by J. Fecunda

This month *Yes, We Believe Magazine* is celebrating six months of life (existence). I'd like to say something in respect to this. Sometimes we meet people and just don't know what role they will have in our path, and this is just great, for this time, I'm going to say just how Ryan and Steve played a part in faith of seeing and encouraging our vision of the *Yes, We Believe Magazine*. They are both home designers in a construction building, both qualified carpenters. I have worked with them. They shared their knowledge, and so did I (mine is based on Jesus). So at times, when it got too much for them, I believe the Spirit guided them, for God knows His people and how to go about giving them a chance. They are free to have a spiritual rebirth with consciousness; they are free, of course, to accept or decline this. *Isn't God awesome and great?*

Well, let me not get too much off course with this testimony. We worked and talked and became acquainted to some truths about the spiritual world. So I've shared my thoughts about having this magazine, and yes, strange as it seems, they both bought it and became the first two subscribers of the *Yes, We Believe Magazine*, with a whole-year subscription. They are the first readers of the magazine, by each one giving a twenty-pound note for stamps. I'd like to believe if they ever give their heart to Jesus, I will see them in heaven, but I'll say this instead, 'Guys, I know it's hard to get involved with the Lord because of the confusion there is in this world. Jesus is power, and to understand this, *one* has got to believe in faith, just like you drink a cool beer or wine. I encourage you with this: drink it in faith in the name of Jesus and see your life. People will start telling you as to confirm the miracle. If you fear, read the Bible, Romans chapter 8! Last but not least, I hope you continue reading. Hey, may God bless you both in the name of Jesus, Lord and King of Kings.'

Thank you to Mr Ryan Parker and Steve Rose from us servants of the Lord Jesus Christ—Jorge, Veneranda, and Sarah Fecunda.

James

OUR JOURNEY WITH JESUS
by V. Pallara Fecunda

Dear Sarah,

We left Italy almost two years ago—your father, me, and you too—because I was already pregnant. We have been in many different places, like Germany, Holland, France, Spain, Portugal, London, Israel, and London, again where you were born on 1 February 2001. We travelled only by the grace of God Almighty, and I have many stories to share with you and with the readers of *Yes, We Believe Magazine*. We met many people with whom we spoke about our faith and love of Jesus. We shared with them the good news and our spiritual walk in Jesus' name. It was not important, like now, if the meeting was short or long; the name of Jesus was proclaimed and shared not by our power or strength but by the power of the Holy Spirit.

I remember I was seven months pregnant when we went to Israel. (During my pregnancy, I only saw the doctor the first month in Holland and the last one here in London. It was our choice. We could not see a doctor in every place, and God Almighty is the best doctor.) Many things happened in Israel. One of these I want to share with you today. We were in Jerusalem when your father said, 'Today we will go to Bethlehem.' When we went to the bus station, it was not a real bus station but a place with many little buses. We asked about Bethlehem, and someone said to us, 'You cannot go to Bethlehem because the town is closed for the war.' We thought, *If God wants, we will be there today.* God wanted, and we found a bus with a cheap price for Bethlehem (the price was so low, only five shekel for two people, because in those days, Bethlehem was not touristy). The bus took a different route than usual because the main road was closed. The trip was bumpy, and your father said,

'Please, we have a pregnant woman on board!' They all looked at us like we were out of our mind to say what your father said.

I saw the soldiers with the machine guns stop other cars, but not the one we were on. Maybe they knew already the driver. In that moment, your father was talking about our faith in Jesus with a Muslim man. He liked how your father spoke, and when we arrived in Bethlehem, he showed us the right way to the centre of the town. He helped us with my bag and bought us a Coca-Cola. We gave him our first cassette. Later we shared our faith and gave a cassette to a Catholic priest. He told us about the situation there with the war, and the town was empty for this reason. A little bit later, we went in a tourist office, where we also left a cassette. For us, the cassette is a blessing of God, made with the guidance of the Holy Spirit. This is our faith that its music brings joy and healing by the power of the Holy Spirit. We left Bethlehem that same day. We could not stay there because the hotels were closed, and we could not sleep on the street because of the curfew, so your father decided to go back in Jerusalem. But we did not know how because there were no buses to return. We walked in faith that God was with us, and we saw a little bus. In the bus, the driver asked us why we were there with that situation. The bus was full of Muslim people. Your father spoke the truth about our faith, and he gave the driver a cassette to say thanks because he took us in his bus. The driver put the cassette and turned up the volume. The cassette started with the first song, 'Let's All Praise Jesus'. Everyone in the bus stopped to talk. I thought, *Oh my God!* We arrived in Jerusalem and from there to Tel-Aviv with the grace of God.

Thank You, Lord. Psalm 23:4 GNT says, 'Even I go through the deepest darkness, I will not be afraid, Lord for you are with me. Your Shepherd's rod and staff protect me.'

(To be continued next month.)

Thomas

PRAYER

People to pray for:

- David of KCD store (London)
- Maggi and his endeavour, a pizzeria named Armatura del Re
- Efesini 6:10 (Italy)
- Miguel Buen Viaje a Columbia (He will be the first to carry our faith, our magazine, and our music to Colombia.)
- Ashlin (Barclay Bank)
- Pastor F. Citarella and his congregation (Italy)
- Pastor J. Blindelling and his congregation (Curaçao)
- Matteo Placentino and his family (Italy)
- Chiara Placentino (*La nostra preghiera e' semplice e umile se tu chiami il nome di Gesu' e l'accetti con il cuore, Gesu' non ti lascera' mai*)
- Ryan Parker and Steve
- Rose (London)
- Council of Hammersmith and Fulham Borough

If you know how to pray this, then please do!

If you don't know and wish to pray, do this prayer:

'Jesus, I believe You are the Son of God who raised again and lived in the consciousness of man to teach and help us on our redemtion and salvation.

Holy Spirit of Jesus, You are welcome in my temple [mind, body, and soul]. I will consider this done. Thank You, in the name of Jesus. Amen.

After this, just consider this a call made to Jesus and say, "Please help my brothers [call the names written].'

London N. 6 July 2002

Freely you have received, freely give! (Matthew 10:8 NIV)

YES, WE BELIEVE MAGAZINE!

INTRODUCTION

Matthias

This magazine will be based on twelve topics every month as we await the arrival of our Saviour, Jesus Christ. Walk with Jesus, our Saviour, as He lives through us with all His glory, sacrifices, riches, love, ministry, and prayer. God bless you as you take the time to see and read *Yes, We Believe Magazine!* It is unveiled to those who are being saved. It is written simply and humbly. All the glory to Jesus.

Bartholomew

Multitudes who sleep in the dust of the earth will awake: some to everlasting life, others to shame and everlasting contempt. Those who are wise will shine like the brightness of the heavens, and those who lead many to righteousness, like the stars for ever and ever. But as for you, continue in what you have learned and have become convinced of, because you know those from whom you learned it, and how from infancy you have know the Holy Scriptures, which are able to make you wise for salvation through faith in Christ Jesus. All Scripture is God-breathed and is useful for teaching, rebuking, correcting and training in righteousness, so that the man of God may be thoroughly equipped for every good work. Who is wise? He will realise those things. Who is discerning? He will understand them. The ways of the Lord are right; the righteous walk in them, but the rebellious stumble in them.

Daniel 12:2–3; 2 Timothy 3:14–17; Hosea 14:9

Founder:
Jehovah Adonao Shaddai
Jesus Christ
Holy Spirit
12 Apostles
All the Holy Bible that worked through us your servants: Jorge, Veneranda, and Sarah Fecunda

For subscription: fecundaj@hotmail.com

Philip

OPINION ON THIS QUESTION
by J. Fecunda

WHAT IS YOUR OPINION ON PRAYER?

Let's look at what Jesus taught His disciples when He was asked this question! 'Lord teach us to pray' (Luke 11:1–4 NIV). I always refer to the Bible for I believe; however, the Lord's teaching through the Bible is interesting to see because it shows how great is God's unfailing love (Luke 11:13). Here is where people have a misconception of prayer and never get anything after their prayer, for they have no idea what was given. The Bible teaches: ask and you will be given. How can we receive when we have no conscience of what we have received after asking? For there is also written: 'Seek first the Kingdom of the Lord God and all will be given to you.' All the Bible is written by many of different people and walks to show how great our God is. An example of what I'm saying is this: We are given a book with code to use or a map to walk by, but we don't familiarise ourselves with it. And then we hear of someone or feel the need to pray. Whom do you pray to? What do you know of him? How would you know you've been given what you prayed for without having read or shown the ways to receive what you've asked for?

This is just a simple example of how God is merciful with us. He has given special blessings to those who knew how to have and keep close relation with the Spirit of Jesus, our Lord! The Spirit is given by God—unlimited! For if we can understand or grasp this, it's written: 'In the beginning, God created the heavens and the earth. Now the earth was formless and empty, darkness was over the surface of the deep, and the Spirit of God was hovering over the waters.' Now we can understand so much more as we read the Bible, then we can understand how come I speak of knowing what we pray for, as it's written in the book of Luke 11:13 NIV, 'If you then though you are evil, know how to give good gifts to your children, how much more will your Father in heaven give the Holy Spirit to those who ask him.' And what is given is the Spirit. We can now do everything in Jesus' name, for He overcame *death*; therefore, He is the *master of life* for us whom we believe and ask for His *Spirit* to come and dwell in us.

Okay, now I can say this. It's my opinion that we know what God gives when we pray. This is what we will receive: the Spirit of God, which is holy! As we know, God is almighty; His Spirit is almighty. That's how the Son is almighty for He was raised by the Spirit of God. See how Jesus prayed for Himself (John 17:5). Our Master prayed for His disciples (John 17:15–18). Jesus prayed for all believers (John 17:21, 26). Understand, this is in Spirit. Read all of John 17 if you like. I know you are thinking, *So how come some people pray for things and have not received it?* Well, what I can say is, see if you can understand this example: when you pray for something but don't have a relationship with the Almighty through the Spirit, you will probably receive a spiritual awakening by someone whom God will send for this intervention to show you a way to a communicative relationship, but you just wanted what you've prayed for! So you cannot see all this process by God and think, *I've not been heard with my prayer!* My encouragement is that prayer is a relationship with the Spirit of God, which will then guide you to all truths and things of God! I'll show you a prayer in the Bible (Hannah's Prayer) in 1 Samuel 2:1–10 NIV:

> My heart rejoices in the Lord; in the Lord my horn is lifted high. My mouth boasts over my enemies, for I delight in your deliverance. There is no-one holy like the Lord; there is no-one besides you; there is no Rock like our God. Do not keep talking so proudly or let your mouth speak such arrogance, for the Lord is a God who knows, and by him deeds are weighed. The bows of the warriors are broken, but those who stumbled are armed with strength. Those who were full hire themselves out

for food, but those who were hungry hunger no more. She who was barren has borne seven children, but she who has had many sons pines away. The Lord brings death and makes alive; he brings down to the grave and raises up. The Lord sends poverty and wealth; he humbles and he exalts. He raises the poor from the dust and lifts the needy from the ash heap; he seats them with princes and has them inherit a throne of honour. For the foundations of the earth are the Lord's: upon them he has set the world. He will guard the feet of his saints, but the wicked will by silenced in darkness. It is not by strength that one prevails; those who oppose the Lord will be shattered. He will thunder against them from heaven; the Lord will judge the ends of the earth. He will give strength to his king and exalt the horn of his anointed. (*End*)

And this is how Apostle Paul describes the Spirit poured out on him. *Grace* is another word for *Spirit*. 1 Timothy 1:12–17 NIV says, 'I thank Christ Jesus our Lord, who has given me strength, that he considered me faithful, appointing me to his service. Even though I was once a blasphemer and a persecutor and a violent man. I was shown mercy because I acted in ignorance and unbelief. The grace of our Lord Jesus was poured out on me abundantly, along with the faith and love that are in Christ Jesus. Here is a trustworthy saying that deserves full acceptance: Christ Jesus came into the world to save sinners of whom I am the worst. But for that very reason was shown mercy so that in me, the worst of sinners, Christ Jesus might display his unlimited patience as an example for those who would believe on him and receive eternal life. Now to the King, eternal, immortal, invisible, the only God, be honour and glory for ever and ever. Amen.'

The story of Jonah is also interesting to see because it shows how he prayed to the Lord when he was swallowed by a big fish! Jonah 2:1–10 states, 'From inside the fish Jonah prayed to the Lord his God. He said: "In my distress I called to the Lord, and he answered me. From the depths of the grave I called for help, and you listened to my cry. You hurled me into the deep, into the very heart of the seas, and the currents swirled about me; all your waves and breakers swept over me. I said, 'I have been banished from your sight; yet I will look again towards your holy temple.' The engulfing waters threatened me, the deep surrounded me; seaweed was wrapped around my head. To the roots of the mountains I sank down; the earth beneath barred me in for ever. But you brought my life up from the pit, O Lord my God. When my life was ebbing away, I remembered you, Lord, and my prayer rose to you, to your holy temple. Those who cling to worthless idols forfeit the grace that could be theirs. But I, with a song of thanksgiving, will sacrifice to you. What I have vowed I will Make good. Salvation comes from the Lord." And the Lord commanded the fish, and it vomited Jonah on to dry land.'

Let's be real and believe we will receive what we pray for if we know to whom we pray to and how this will be given so we'll know when we have received. Thank You, Jesus. To you be honour and glory, the only mediator of God and man. This is the New Covenant, the living Spirit of Jesus!

James

THE TABERNACLE

In June, we set up the tabernacle of the Lord twice—in the morning in Hammersmith Park, in the Japanese garden, and in the afternoon in King Street (Hammersmith). It was a wonderful day with sunshine. God blessed us with this beautiful day. In Hammersmith Park, we glorified the name of Jesus in the midst of the trees, and we prayed for our 12.000 km of faith, liberation for those who truly seek God. We were in the park alone up on the hill (the Japanese garden), and I realised that it's important to say thanks to God for the life we live and, as my husband says, for the air we breathe. I believe that these things are so simple that we can forget them. We start wanting something more, and we forget the simplicity of God. For example, we build a church for Him, and in the Bible, it's written: 'But the Most High God does not live in houses built by human hands; as the prophet says: Heaven is my throne, says the Lord, and the earth is my footstool. What kind of house would you build for me? Where is the place for me to live in? Did not I myself make all these things?' (Acts 7:48–50 NIV).

I encourage everyone to praise God not only in the church. I know sometimes it's difficult in front of unbelievers to glorify God; I know because I felt this sensation, and you can find the story in this issue of *Yes, We Believe Magazine*. For this reason, I can say that if we have fear, it's because we don't have enough faith that God is with us and in us and also in other people. For a church is a building where the man, made in God's likeness, congregate to glorify God in us, all in the name of Jesus, and this is all in faith. Let me continue my testimony of the Lord's tabernacle held on the first of June. When we finished in Hammersmith Park, God gave us a beautiful time in the playground with our daughter, Sarah. In the afternoon, as I said, we went in King Street. We set up the tabernacle in front of McDonalds. A guy with his girlfriend stopped and said, 'Are you buskers?' I said, 'No, we are praising God.' And he said, 'Oh, sorry!' But after a few seconds, he came back and said, 'Hey, I also praise God, and I want to give you something.' He gave us 70p, and we shared with him our faith. We gave him our cassette and our *Yes, We Believe Magazine*.

Judas or Thaddaeus

PRAYER

People to pray for:

- Claudio, Theresa, and Lucas Gomes (Alaska)
- Pallara Giovanni e Rachele *che Dio vi benedica siete i nuovi abbonati di Yes, We Believe Magazine* (Italy)
- Steve and Maggie from Safeway (London)
- Margaret Ajinusi (Thank you. We give you our riches—a prayer. May the Lord show this in kindness. Amen.) (London)
- Anis, Nawal, Rajaa' Barhoum and the House of Light (Israel)
- For Miami, the school of Curtis Tucker and his family (USA)

If you know how to pray this, then please do!

If you don't know and wish to pray, do this prayer:

'Jesus, I believe You are the Son of God who raised again and lived in the consciousness of man to teach and help us on our redemtion and salvation.

Holy Spirit of Jesus, You are welcome in my temple [mind, body, and soul]. I will consider this done. Thank You, in the name of Jesus. Amen.

After this, just consider this a call made to Jesus and say, "Please help my brothers [call the names written].'

THE TABERNACLE

EVERY FIRST OF THE MONTH WE HOLD BY FAITH THE TABERNACLE TO SAY THANK YOU AND TO CALL THE PRESENCE OF THE <u>LORD JESUS CHRIST</u>.
OUR FAITH IS THAT THIS BRINGS HEALINGS, JOY AND ALL THAT THE HOLY SPIRIT REVEALS TO THOSE OF FAITH.

GOD BLESS YOU IN THE NAME OF JESUS, OUR SAVIOUR.

Simon

OUR JOURNEY WITH JESUS
by V. Fecunda

Dear Sarah,

   I remember when we left Spain and went to Portugal. We arrived from Ciudad de Rodrigo (Spain) to a little place (I don't remember the name), the border between the two countries. We did not have nothing, only one thousand lire (Italian lire). We tried to change this money, but the teller at the bureau change said, 'I cannot change this money because I have to take the commission, so I cannot give you the rest because with this money you can pay only the commission.' So we did not have money. We arrived there, of course, with the grace of God, and we had faith that the same grace could bring us to Portugal. All the money we had we received by grace in praising on the street. The place was small, and the people there started to look at us like we were crazy because we wanted to go to Portugal but we did not have money.
   Your father did not feel the guide of the Holy Spirit to praise there. So we thought that we could ask for a lift. I remember a policeman said to us, 'You can be here for two months, but no one will give you a lift.' We started with our thumb up, asking for a lift, and the people there were very curious to see our failure. God Almighty is bigger than every human beings thought. After one hour or more, your father prayed strongly to our Lord Jesus, and ±5 minutes later, something happened—a big and beautiful car (a new Audi 100) stopped. We were so happy, and your father spoke in Italian to the driver and said, 'Metto le borse dietro.' I thought, *Why is he speaking Italian?* He did not know why. Anyway, this gentleman who gave us the lift that day was Italian from Milan. If I remember well, his name was Luciano, and he was working for an Italian car company. He was bringing the car to Aveiro (Portugal).

We said, 'Thanks, you are an angel. God answered our prayer.' We spoke about our faith, and your father sang for him in the car. We did not say nothing about our financial situation, and he gave us ten thousand scudos. Hallelujah! With this money, we paid the train ticket from Aveiro to Lisbon, and when we arrived in Lisbon the day after in the early morning, we could pay also the hotel for three or four days. We sent to Luciano our first cassette from Lisbon. *God is good*, He is almighty, and no one can stop His will.

> How great is your goodness, which you can have stored up for those who fear you, which you bestow in the sight of men on those who take refuge in you. Love the Lord, all his saints! The Lord preserves the faithful, but the proud he pays back in full. Be strong and take heart, all you who hope in the Lord. (Psalm 31:19, 23–24 NIV)

> Because he loves me, says the Lord, I will rescue him; I will protect him, for he acknowledges my name. He will call upon me, and I will answer him; I will be with him in trouble, I will deliver him and honour him. With long life will I satisfy him and show him my salvation. (Psalm 91:14–16 NIV)

Andrew

SARAH, PRINCESS OF GOD

The true name of Tutu is Sarah. For this month, I decided to use her true name because I thought that if I speak the truth, I cannot use an imaginary name. We (my husband and I) called Sarah Tutu before she was born, in the last months of my pregnancy, when we felt more her movements. When we started *Yes, We Believe Magazine*, we thought it was a nice idea to use this name. But now with my growth, I changed my thought, and my husband agrees with me. It's important for us to speak the truth before God.

SARAH, THE PRINCESS OF GOD AND THE BIRDS

Sarah likes birds. Every week, once or twice a week, she goes with the family to the river to bring bread to the birds. She calls the birds Ka. She is so happy when her father says, 'Today, we'll go to Ka.' Always her answer is 'Kaaaaaaaah' with joy. The Ka (birds) are happy too to see Sarah and the family with the bread. They started to recognise the family. In sharing this story, a verse of the Bible comes to my mind, Matthew 6:26 GNT, which says, 'Look at birds: they do not sow seeds, gather a harvest and put in barns; yet your Father in heaven takes care of them! Aren't you worth much more than birds?' How does God Almighty take care of them? I'm sure in many different ways. What do you think, reader? Is it possible that God Almighty use also us people to feed the birds? I think it's possible, and it's wonderful to think that this family can be used by God to feed the birds, like many other people. And we should remember also that we are made in the likeness of God (Genesis 1:27). So God is in us, but how much of God is in us? Like my husband says, it depends on our consciousness of God in us, because we have also evil in us.

Often I thought that the believers are not so much interested in animals. I cannot understand why! If you know the answer, let me know, because for me it's really strange. God ordered Noah to take into the boat every kind of animal and bird in order to keep them alive. 'Take along all kinds of food for you and for them' (Genesis 6:19–21). In Isaiah 11:6–8 GNT, it's written: 'Wolves and sheep will live together in peace, and leopards will lie down with young goats. Calves and lion cubs will feed together, and little children will take care of them. Cows and bears will eat together, and their calves and cubs will lie down in peace. Lions will eat straw as cattle do. Even a baby will not be harmed if it plays near a poisonous snake.' From these verses, I understood the love of God for the animals. I thank God for Sarah's growing love for the animals and pray that with God's guidance, this continues to grow as the stories of the princess of God continues.

Thomas

THE SPIRIT OF JESUS
by J. Fecunda

Those who have in mind the things of the Lord will see the pouring out of the Lord's Spirit in our story and testimony of faith in glorifying the name of Lord Jesus on the street or open air. Oh, if you want to know if this is biblical, I encourage you to read Psalm 107:22, Romans 3:21–24, Psalm 145, and yes, almost all of Psalms are saying to praise the Lord. So my ministry, according to the guidance of the Holy Spirit, is to do just this, and all that the Lord Jesus wants as my temple belongs to Him—yes, my temple, not the temple built by the hands of man! The Lord did say as His Spirit spoke through Apostle Peter in Acts 2:14–24 NIV, 'Then Peter stood up with the Eleven, raised his voice and addressed the crowd: Fellow Jews and all of you who live in Jerusalem, let me explain this to you; listen carefully to what I say. These men are not drunk, as you suppose. It's only nine in the morning! No, this is what was spoken by the prophet Joel: "In the last days, God says, I will pour out my Spirit on all people. Your sons and daughters will prophesy, your young men will see visions, your old men will dream dreams. Even on my servants, both men and women, I will pour out my Spirit in those days, and they will prophesy. I will show wonders in the heaven above and signs on the earth below, blood and fire and billows of smoke. The sun will be turned to darkness and the moon to blood before the coming of the great and glorious day of the Lord. And everyone who calls on the name of the Lord will be saved." Men of Israel, listen to this: Jesus of Nazareth was a man accredited by God to you by miracles, wonders and signs, which God did among you through him, as you yourselves know. This man was handed over to you by God's purpose and foreknowledge; and you, with the help of wicked men, put him to death by nailing him to the cross. But God raised him from the dead, freeing him from the agony of death, because it was impossible for death to keep its hold on him.'

Here are testimonies of where this pouring out of God's Holy Spirit took place: Primrose Hill, bank, Stoke-on-Trent, Charing Cross Station, Shepherd's Bush, and Earl's Court. In these places, the praising took place.

Primrose Hill. The day after the tabernacle, the second of June, we went to praise God on Primrose hill—from Hammersmith to Camden Town to Primrose Hill. In the bus from Hammersmith, we met an Italian graphic designer. We started to talk because Jorge and I were speaking in Italian, and he asked, 'Are you Italian?' So, the conversation started, and after a few minutes, my husband was speaking to him about our faith and life. The gentleman was interested to know how faith in Jesus works in a family like us. After sharing some information, we gave him our work of faith—a cassette and a *Yes, We Believe Magazine.* We arrived in Primrose Hill in the afternoon, and many people were there on that lovely day. We went on the hill, and my husband said, 'We will praise here.' I said, 'What?' I was afraid. It was strange because we praise God on the street in the presence of many people, but that day, I thought, *these people are relaxing. Maybe we will disturb them.* What ignorance! How could I imagine that? Thank God for His mercy; He showed me my incredulity. Many people enjoyed the praise. Of course, God has joy when His children are praising His holy name. We have been there maybe for one hour and a half. I learnt that day that it's important to trust completely in God Almighty, who said, 'Never will I leave you. Never will I forsake you.' So, what can man do to me? Nothing. I understood that even in a place where I thought is unusual for praising God, the presence of God is also there, and if I trust in Him, He will give me the strength through His Holy Spirit. That day, I saw in actual fact the manifestation of the Holy Spirit on the people: the peace, the tranquillity, the joy, the freedom. Thank You, God, for your teaching. Thank You, Jesus, for the Holy Spirit.

Bank. This day, the England football supporters were louder than us at the beginning of our praising. Until the Spirit took control and for a half hour or more, we praised, and the Lord made them and us happy, even with the team winning, as we understood later. God is great; in Him, there is no favouritism. If we all breathe air and have life, this is one of the awesome gifts of God, and it's free for all, even to those without denomination. Thank God that no one but the Almighty controls this.

Stoke-on-Trent. This is a place where if you had asked me if I have heard of it, I would have said 'No, where is this place?' But God Almighty had blessings for them, and He sent us His faithful servants that He calls friends to deliver His grace by praising. We already said we believe, and we see that this brings joy, healing, and all that the Lord does when we call the presence of the Holy Spirit for those that the Spirit wants to reach. Okay, we know that if you are a reader with faith, you can understand this greatness through faith and belief in Christ Jesus. However, we may have to say a bit more for those who don't believe and or have little or no faith in Jesus, our Saviour. If by now you are still reading, you will have more faith and belief from now on in your life! I challenge you as I say this prayer for you in the name of Jesus: Lord, I've been asking and interceding in prayer for those who believe. This person reading right now have not stopped reading, though I cannot see this and will have to believe with all my heart, so please touch and bless this person right now. Father, I pray that they will believe and have more faith from now on. O Lord, please convince and confirm this to them (him/her), in the name of Jesus, I pray. Amen. In this town of Stoke-on-Trent, people have never seen us or knew what was to happen that day there. We arrived and went straight in the centre as this was the flow of the town, but the exact place only God knew. We walked—the wind was strong—and I thought, *I will see if where we were to praise would be a place where we can set up everything without having it blown away.* For now, we lay a piece of carpet we call joy on the ground, and we also have a box with *Yes, We Believe Magazine*, which people can now take for free, as we are also sharing this along with our praising. And last but not least, we have a plastic poster sign that we stick with Bostik to let people just passing by get a quick understanding of what we are doing. We have written: 'Our faith is to call the presence of Lord Jesus by praising. We are not praising for profit or peddling the Word of God for profit. May God Almighty bless you as you pass by in grace of the Holy Spirit of Jesus Christ. Amen.' So this is enough reason to hope for a good place to praise where the wind would not blow away the things we have. I must say, we humans in our service to the Lord Almighty are challenged to have balanced mind and still be guided by the Spirit and not think of things. He wants us to think! And after thinking, we present every thought to Him and not worry about it at all for it is His will we are to fulfil. (Great and awesome like the air we breathe, that's God Almighty.) You see, everything will unfold, like the day will have a bright start in the morning that ends by night. So we started praising and ended—only this time, for the first time in my praising on the street, the Lord gave Stoke-on-Trent a revelation out of the Scriptures, as I read what was given through the Holy Spirit in Luke 19:28–31. Thank You, Jesus. Lord, thank You for the miracle of that day. Thank you for those people who came close and shook hands, the lady who gave her change, the family of three that gave and received a cassette and a *Yes, We Believe Magazine*, the girl who came close and received a prophecy that she was taken by this and said 'I will do!', the policeman who did not come close but left and smiled, and the many others who did not know what was happening but were taken by the intervention of the Lord our God as He poured out the Spirit of blessing, love, peace, repentance, prophecy, revelation, and things that only faith in Jesus' Spirit can explain.

Charing Cross Station. In London on Saturday, a day that we just had no clue what was going on in the city, I was inspired to go and praise at Charing Cross Station. Well, we got ready and got on the bus for the city bus no. 10. We enjoyed sitting upstairs in the bus for Sarah loved it, and we do as well. That day, the Lord God had a surprise for us. As we were approaching our stop on the Oxford Street, we heard people shouting, screaming. At that moment, from the height in the bus, we saw at the same level, for it was the same bus but open. Michael Jackson and a large crowd were running after the bus. We thought, *Glory to Jesus. Look how this man is at the same level of the bus (height), and there are people making an idol out of him for the recognition the world gave him.* Surely to God, he is just another being who breathes the air God gives to all, and man is still blind to this wisdom of God. I'm glad, and we give glory to Jesus, God, Jehovah, and the Holy Spirit. Well, after that surprise, we went to glorify and call the presence of the Spirit, not knowing about football. England was playing again, and we walked through the many thousands of people who were in Leicester Square. Perfect timing as at that same moment, the football game was over! We heard the shouts 'England! England!' As that was not enough, we walked in the same direction with the Grenadier of Glasgow. The joy of everyone was loud and overwhelming. I said to my wife, 'Would it be nice if they praised God like this?' (Well, in our saying of what we understand, man is made in the likeness of God, so I should really say God's consciousness, not of the idolatry, fanaticism, and the chain events to this nature of events, which is here today and gone tomorrow. Remember, I'm not against those who play football. I praise God and encourage faith. This is spiritual food. So we praised and was at one point again was louder than those who was shouting for England. I believe God's Spirit again took over us and them as we praised. Thank You, Jesus.

Shepherd's Bush. Today again, we spent one hour of pouring out the Spirit of God on non-believers and believers. Yes, this is how God does it through people like us. Many hallelujahs were said today at the open space between the traffic lights and the Shepherd's Bush station. Glory to Jesus.

Earl's Court. On 27/06/2002, in the small street in front of the station concluded this month's pouring of the Spirit of Jesus. How great are your works Lord. Thank You for having us live through Your work of faith and to testify about them to the honour and praise of Your Son and our Saviour, Jesus Christ. Thank You!

Matthew

NEWS FROM THE BIBLE

As for you, you were dead in your transgressions and sins, in which you used to live when you followed the ways of this world and of the ruler of the kingdom of the air, the spirit who is now at work in those who are disobedient. All of us also lived among them at one time, gratifying the cravings of our sinful nature and following its desires and thoughts. Like the rest, we were by nature objects of wrath. But because of his great love for us, God who is rich in mercy, made us alive with Christ even when we were dead in transgression, it is by grace you have been saved. And God raised us up with Christ and seated us with him in the heavenly realms in Christ Jesus, in order that in the coming ages he might show the incomparable riches of his grace, expressed in his kindness to us in Christ Jesus. For it is by grace you have been saved, through faith and this not from yourselves, it is the gift of God, not by works, so that no-one can boast. For we are God's workmanship, created in Christ Jesus to do good works, which God prepared in advance for us to do. Therefore, remember that formerly you who are Gentiles by birth and called uncircumcised by those who call themselves the circumcision (that done in the body by the hands of men) remember that at time you were separate from Christ, excluded from citizenship in Israel and foreigners to the covenants of the promise, without hope and without God in the world. But now in Christ Jesus you who once were far away have been brought near through the blood of Christ. For he himself is our peace, who has made the two one and has destroyed the barrier, the dividing wall of hostility, by abolishing in his flesh the law with its commandments and regulations. His purpose was to create in himself one new man out of the two, thus making peace, and in this one body to reconcile both of them to God through the cross, by which he put to death their Hostility. He came and preached peace to you who were far away and peace to those who were near. For through him we both have access to the Father by one Spirit. Consequently, you are no longer foreigners and aliens, but fellow citizens with God's people and members of God's household, built on the foundation of the apostles and prophets, with Christ Jesus himself as the chief cornerstone. In him the whole building is joined together and rises to become a holy temple in the Lord. And in him you too are being built together to become a dwelling in which God lives by his Spirit.

Ephesians 2 NIV

Peter

SIXTH SPIRITUAL LETTER

6th SPIRITUAL LETTER

The wall of the city had twelve foundations, and on them were the names of the twelve apostles of the Lamb.

Do you not know that he who unites himself with a prostitute is one with her in body? For it is said, "The two will become one flesh." But he who unites himself with the Lord is one with him in Spirit.

Flee from sexual immorality. All other sins a man commits are outside his body, but he who sins sexually sins against his own body.

Do you not know that your body is a temple of the Holy Spirit, who is in you, whom you have received from God? You are not your own; you were bought at a price. Therefore, honour God with your body.

In the beginning God created the heavens and the earth. Now the earth was formless and empty, darkness was over the surface of the deep, and the Spirit of God was hovering over the waters.

Brothers, I could not address you as spiritual but as wordly. For since there is jealousy and quarrelling among you are you not wordly? Are you not acting like mere men? For when one says, "I follow Paul", and another, "I follow Apollos", are you not mere men?

Blessed is the one who reads the words of this prophecy and blessed are those who hear it and take to heart what is written in it, because the time is near.

Don't grumble against each other, brothers, or you will be judged. The judge is standing at the door! Brothers, as an example of patience in the face of suffering, take the prophets who spoke in the name of the Lord.

Therefore, say to the house of Israel, this is what the Sovereign Lord says: Repent! Turn from your idols and renounce all your detestable practices! When any Israelite or any alien living in Israel separates himself from me and sets up idols in his heart and puts a wicked stumbling-block before his face and then goes to a prophet to enquire of me, I the Lord will answer him myself.

We know that anyone born of God does not continue to sin; the one who was born of God keeps him safe, and the evil one cannot harm him.

We know that we are children of God, and that the whole world is under the control of the evil one. We know also that the son of God has come and has given us understanding, so that we may know him who is true. And we are in him who is true, even in his Son Jesus Christ. He is true God and Eternal Life. Dear children, keep yourselves from idols.

Therefore, prepare your minds for action, be self-controlled, set your hope fully on the Grace to be given you when Jesus Christ is revealed.

As obedient children do not conform to the evil desires you had when lived in ignorance. But just as he who called you is holy, so be holy in all you do; for it is written: "Be holy, because I am holy."

Unlike so many, we do not peddle the word of God for profit. On the contrary, in Christ we speak before God with sincerity, like men sent from God.

Dear friends, do not believe every spirit, but test the spirits to see whether they are from God, because many false prophets have gone out into the world.

This is how you can recognise the Spirit of God: Every spirit that acknowledges that Jesus Christ has come in the flesh is from God, but every spirit that does not acknowledge Jesus is not from God. This is the spirit of the antichrist, which you have heard is coming and even now is already in the world.

You, dear children, are from God and overcome them, because the one who is in you is greater than the one who is in the world. They are from the world and therefore speak from the viewpoint of the world, and the world listens to them. We are from God, and whoever knows God listens to us; but whoever is not from God does not listen to us. This is how we recognise the spirit of truth and the spirit of falsehood.

For everyone who calls on the name of the Lord will be saved. How, then, can they call on the one they have not believed in? And how can they believe in the one of whom they have not heard? And how can they hear without someone preaching to them? And how can they preach unless they are sent? As it is written, "How beautiful are the feet of those who bring good news!"

Don't you know that you yourselves are God's temple and that God's Spirit lives in you? If anyone destroys God's temple, God will destroy him; for God's temple is sacred, and you are that temple.

Do not deceive yourselves. If anyone of you thinks he is wise by the standards of this age, he should become a "Fool" so that he may, become wise. For the wisdom of the world is foolishness in God's sight. As it is written: "He catches the wise in their craftiness"; and again, "The Lord knows that the thoughts of the wise are futile."

We are fools for Christ, but you are so wise in Christ! We are weak, but you are strong! You are honoured, we are dishonoured! For it seems to me that God has put us apostles on display at the end of the procession, like men condemned to die in the arena. We have been made a spectacle to the whole universe, to angels as well to men.

To this very hour we go hungry and thirsty, we are in rags, we are brutally treated, we are homeless. We work hard with our own hands. When we are cursed, we bless; when we are persecuted, we endure it; when we are slandered, we answer kindly. Up to this moment we have become the scum of the earth, the refuse of the world.

For who makes you different from anyone else? What do you have that you did not receive? And if you did receive it, why do you boast as though you did not? Already you have all you want! Already you have become rich! You have become kings and that without us! How I wish that you really had become kings so that we might be kings with you! Dear friends, let us love one another, for love comes from God. Everyone who loves has been born of God and knows God. Whoever does not love does not know God, because God is love.

We know that we live in him and he in us, because he has given us of his Spirit. And we have seen and testify that the Father has sent his Son to be the Saviour of the world. No-one can come to me unless the Father who sent me draws him, and I will raise him up at the last day. It is written in the Prophets: "They will all be taught by God."

Everyone who listens to the Father and learns from him comes to me. No-one has seen the Father except the one who is from God; only he has seen the Father.

I tell you the truth, he who believes has everlasting life. I am the bread of life. Your forefathers ate the manna in the desert, yet they died. But here is the bread that comes down from heaven, which a man may eat and not die.

The Spirit gives life; the flesh counts for nothing. The words I have spoken to you are Spirit and they are life. Yet there are some of you who do not believe.

For Jesus had known from the beginning which of them did not believe and who would betray him. He went on to say, "This is why I told you that no-one can come to me unless the Father has enabled him."

Whoever claims to live in him must walk as Jesus did. If we claim we have not sinned, we make him out to be a liar and his word has no place in our lives.

If you forgive anyone, I also forgive him. And what I have forgiven, if there was anything to forgive, I have forgiven in the sight of Christ for your sake, in order that satan might not outwit us. For we are not unaware of his schemes.

The reason I wrote to you was to see if you would stand the test and be obedient in everything. But I have a mind as well as you; I am not inferior to you. Who does not know all these things?

Let him who does wrong continue to do wrong; let him who is vile continue to be vile; let him who does right continue to do right; and let him who is holy continue to be holy.

Jesus answered: "Watch out that no-one deceives you. For many will come in my name, claiming, I am the Christ, and will deceive many. You will hear of wars and rumours of wars but see to it that you are not alarmed. Such things must happen, but the end is still to come. Nation will rise against nation, and kingdom against kingdom. There will be famines and earthquakes in various places. All these are the beginning of birth pains. Then you will be handed over to be persecuted and put to death, and you will be hated by all nations because of me at that time many will turn away from the faith and will betray and hate each other, and many false prophets will appear and deceive many people.

Because of the increase of wickedness, the love of most will grow cold, but he who stands firm to the end will be saved. And this Gospel of the Kingdom will be preached in the whole world as a testimony to all nations, and then the end will come. So, when you see standing in the holy place "The abomination that causes desolation", spoken of through the prophet Daniel (Let the reader understand), he will confirm a covenant with many for one "Seven". In the middle of "The seven" he will put an end to sacrifice and offering. And on a wig of the temple he will set up an abomination that causes desolation, until the end that is decreed is poured out on him. They will bear their guilt; the prophet will be as guilty as the one who consults him.

Do not love the world or anything in the world. If anyone loves the world, the love of the Father is not in him. For everything in the world, the cravings of sinful man, the lust of his eyes and the boasting of what he has and does, comes not from the Father but from the world. The world and its desires pass away, but the man who does the will of God lives for ever.

Be patient, then brothers, until the Lord's coming. See how the farmer waits for the land to yield its valuable crop and how patient he is for the autumn and spring rains. You too, be patient and stand firm, because the Lord's coming is near.

Outside are the dogs, those who practise magic arts, the sexually immoral, the murderers, the idolaters and everyone who loves and practises falsehood. As you know, we consider blessed those who have persevered. You have heard of Job's perseverance and have seen what the Lord finally brought about. The Lord is full of compassion and mercy.

Since you call on a Father who judges each man's work impartially, live your lives as strangers here in reverent fear. By standing firm you will gain life.

GLORY TO JESUS.

Revelation 21: 14; 1 Corinthians 6: 16-20; Genesis 1: 1, 2; 1 Corinthians 3: 1-4; Revelation 1: 3; James 5: 9, 10; Ezekiel 14: 6, 7; 1 John 5: 18-21; 1 Peter 1: 13-16; 2 Corinthians 2: 17; 1 John 4: 1-6; Romans 10: 13-15; 1 Corinthians 3: 16-20; 4: 10, 9, 11-13, 7, 8; 1 John 4: 7, 8, 13, 14; John 6: 44-50, 63-65; 1 John 2: 6; 1: 10; 2 Corinthians 2: 10, 11, 9; Job 12: 3; Revelation 22: 11; Matthew 24: 4-15; Daniel 9: 27; Ezekiel 14: 10; 1 John 2: 15-17; James 5: 7, 8; Revelation 22: 15; James 5: 11; 1 Peter 1: 17; 1 Luke 21: 19.

London N. 7 August 2002

Freely you have received, freely give! (Matthew 10:8 NIV)

YES, WE BELIEVE MAGAZINE

INTRODUCTION

Matthias

This magazine will be based on twelve topics every month as we await the arrival of our Saviour, Jesus Christ. Walk with Jesus, our Saviour, as He lives through us with all His glory, sacrifices, riches, love, ministry, and prayer. God bless you as you take the time to see and read *Yes, We Believe Magazine*! It is unveiled to those who are being saved. It is written simply and humbly. All the glory to Jesus.

Founder:
Jehovah Adonai Shaddai
Jesus Christ
The Holy Spirit
12 Apostles

All the Holy Bible that worked through us your servants: Jorge, Veneranda, and Sarah Fecunda

For Subscription: fecundaj@hotmail.com

SEVENTH SPIRITUAL LETTER

Bartholomew

And do this, understanding the present time. The hour has come for you to wake up from your slumber, because our salvation is nearer now than when we first believed

The night is nearly over; the day is almost here. So, let us put aside the deeds of darkness and put on the armour of light.

Put to death, therefore, whatever belongs to your earthly nature: sexual immorality, impurity, lust, evil desires and greed, which is idolatry. Because of these, the wrath of God is coming on those who are disobedient.

You used to walk in these ways, in the life you once lived, but now you must rid yourselves of all such things as these: anger, rage, malice, slander and filthy language from your lips.

Do not lie to each other, since you have taken off your old self with its practices and have put on the new self, which is being renewed in knowledge in the image of its Creator.

Therefore, since we are God's offspring, we should not think that the divine being is like gold or silver or stone an image made by man's design and skill.

In the past God overlooked such ignorance, but now he commands all people everywhere to repent. For he has set a day when he will judge the world with justice by the man he has appointed. He has given proof of this to all men by raising him from the dead.

What business is it of mine to judge those outside the church? Are you not to judge those inside? God will judge those outside. "Expel the wicked man from among you."

Jesus answered; the work of God is this: to believe in the one he has sent. Do not work for food that spoils, but for food that endures to eternal life, which the Son of Man will give you. On him God the Father has placed his seal of approval.

Then Jesus declared, I am the bread of life. He who comes to me will never go hungry, and he who believes in me will never be thirsty. But as I told you, you have seen me and still you do not believe.

For I have come down from heaven not to do my will but to do the will of him who sent me, that I shall lose none of all that he has given me but raise them up at the last day.

The Spirit gives life; the flesh counts for nothing. The words I have spoken to you are Spirit and they are life. Yet there are some of you who do not believe. For Jesus had known from the beginning which of them did not believe and who would betray him.

For what I received I passed on to you as of first importance: that Christ died for our sins according to the Scriptures, that he was buried, that he was raised on the third day according to the Scriptures and that he appeared to Peter, and then to the twelve. After that he appeared to more than five hundred of the brothers at the same time, most of whom are still living, though some fallen asleep.

Then I saw another Angel flying in mid-air, and he had the Eternal Gospel to proclaim to those who live on the earth to every nation, tribe, language and people. He said in a loud voice, "Fear God and give him glory, because the hour of his judgement has come. Worship him who made the heavens, the earth, the sea and the springs of water."

A second Angel followed and said, "Fallen! Fallen is Babylon the great, which made all the nations drink the maddening wine of her adulteries."

A third Angel followed them and said in a loud voice: "If any worships the beast and his image and receives his mark on the forehead or on the hand, he, too will drink of the wine of God's fury, which has been poured full strength into the cup of his wrath. He will be tormented with burning sulphur in the presence of the holy angels and of the lamb. This calls for patient endurance on the part of the saints who obey God's commandments and remain faithful to Jesus."

Then I heard a voice from heaven say, "Write: blessed are the dead who die in the Lord from now on." "Yes" says the Spirit, "They will rest from their labour, for their deeds will follow them."

For the Grace of God that brings salvation has appeared to all men. It teaches us to say "No" to ungodliness and worldly passions, and to live self-controlled, upright and godly lives in the present age, while we wait for the blessed hope, the glorious appearing of our great God and Saviour, Jesus Christ.

But now in Christ Jesus you who once were far away have been brought near through the blood of Christ. But the Counsellor, the Holy Spirit, whom the Father will send in my name, will teach you all things and will remind you of everything I have said to you.

He who descended is the very one who ascended higher than all the heavens, in order to fill the whole universe. It was he who gave some to be apostles, some to be prophets, some to be evangelists, and some to be pastors and teachers, to prepare God's people for works of service, so that the body of Christ may be built up until we all reach unity in the faith and in the knowledge of the Son of God and become mature, attaining to the whole measure of the fullness of Christ.

Jesus answered, "My teaching is not my own. It comes from him who sent me. If anyone chooses to do God's will, he will find out whether my teaching comes from God or whether I speak on my own. He who speaks on his own does so to gain honour for himself, but he who works for the honour of the one who sent him is a man of truth; there is nothing false about him.

Has not Moses given you the law? Yet not one of you keeps the law. Why are you trying to kill me?"

Love does not delight in evil but rejoices with the truth. It always protects, always trusts, always hopes, always perseveres. Love never fails. But where there are prophecies, they will cease; where there are tongues, they will be stilled; where there is knowledge, it will pass away. For we know in part and we prophesy in part, but when perfection comes, the imperfect disappears.

When I was a child, I talked like a child, I thought like a child, I reasoned like a child. When I became a man, I put childish ways

We thank you with encouragement (Acts 17:17).
We remain faithful in Jesus Christ, our Saviour.

Fam. Jorge, Veneranda (wife), and Sarah (daughter) Fecunda

behind me. Now we see but a poor reflection as in a mirror; then we shall see face to face.

Now I know in part; then I shall know fully, even as I am fully known.

And now these three remain: Faith, Hope and Love. But the greatest of these is Love.

I have revealed you to those whom you gave me out of the world. They were yours; you gave them to me, and they have obeyed your word.

Now they know that everything you have given me comes from you. For I gave them the words you gave me, and they accepted them. They knew with certainty that I came from you and they believed that you sent me.

I pray for them. I am not praying for the world, but for those you have given me, for they are yours. All I have is yours, and all you have is mine. And glory has come to me through them.

For you can all prophesy in turn so that everyone may be instructed and encouraged. For God is not a God of disorder but of peace. As in all congregations of the saints, women should remain silent in the churches. They are not allowed to speak, but must be in submission, as the Law says. If they want to enquire about something, they should ask their own husbands at home; for it is disgraceful for a woman to speak in the church.

If anyone speaks in a tongue, two or at the most three should speak, one at a time, and someone must interpret. If there is no interpreter, the speaker should keep quiet in the church and speak to himself and God.

Two or three prophets should speak, and the others should weigh carefully what is said. And if a revelation comes to someone who is sitting down, the first speaker should stop. But everything should be done in a fitting and orderly way.

Rejoice in the Lord always. I will say it again: Rejoice! Let your gentleness be evident to all. The Lord is near. Do not be anxious about anything, but in everything, by prayer and petition, with thanksgiving, present your requests to God. And the peace of God, which transcends all understanding, will guard your hearts and your mind in Christ Jesus.

Finally, brothers, whatever is true, whatever is noble, whatever is right, whatever is pure, whatever is lovely, whatever is admirable, if anything is excellent or praiseworthy, think about such things.

Whatever you have learned or received or heard from me or seen in me put it into practice. And the God of peace will be with you.

My prayer is not that you take them out of the world but that you protect them from the evil one. My prayer is not for them alone. I pray also for those who will believe in me through their message, that all of them may be one.

Father, just as you are in me and I am in you. May they also be in us so that the world may believe that you have sent me.

I pray that you may be active in sharing your faith, so that you will have a full understanding of every good thing we have in Christ.

For we are to God the aroma of Christ among those who are being saved and those who are perishing. To the one we are the smell of death; to the other, the fragrance of life. And who is equal to such a task? He has made us competent as ministers of a new covenant not of the letter but of the Spirit; for the letter kills, but the Spirit gives life.

You show that you are a letter from Christ, the result of our ministry, written not with ink but with the Spirit of the Living God, not on tablets of stone but on tablets of human hearts.

It is written: "I believed; therefore, I have spoken." With that same spirit of faith, we also believe and therefore speak.

We are hard pressed on every side, but not crushed; perplexed, but not in despair; persecuted, but not abandoned; struck down, but not destroyed.

So, we fix our eyes not on what is seen, but on what is unseen. For what is seen is temporary, but what is unseen is eternal.

The god of this age has blinded the minds of unbelievers, so that they cannot see the light of the gospel of the Glory of Christ, who is the image of God. For we do not preach ourselves, but Jesus Christ as Lord, and ourselves as your servants for Jesus' sake.

For God, who said, "Let light shine out of darkness", made his light shine in our hearts to give us the light of the knowledge of the glory of God in the face of Christ.

But we have this treasure in jars of clay to show that this all surpassing power is from God and not from us. If we have been united with him like this in his death, we will certainly also be united with him in his resurrection.

Now if we died with Christ, we believe that we will also live with him. Therefore, since we have been justified through faith, we have peace with God through our Lord Jesus Christ, through whom we have gained access by faith into this grace in which we now stand.

And we rejoice in the hope of the glory of God. Not only so, but we also rejoice in our sufferings, because we know that suffering produces perseverance; perseverance character; and character, hope. And hope does not disappoint us, because God has poured out his love into our hearts by the Holy Spirit, whom he has given us.

His intent was that now through the church, the manifold wisdom of God should be made known to the rulers and authorities in the heavenly realms, according to his eternal purpose which he accomplished in Christ Jesus our Lord.

In him and through faith in him we may approach God with freedom and confidence. I ask you, therefore, not to be discouraged because of my sufferings for you, which are your glory.

I pray that out of his glorious riches he may strengthen you with power through his spirit in your inner being.

But, in your hearts set apart Christ as Lord. Always be prepared to give an answer to everyone who asks you to give the reason for the hope that you have. But do this with gentleness and respect, keeping a clear conscience, so that those who speak maliciously against your good behaviour in Christ may be ashamed of their slander.

Glory to Jesus!

Romans 13:11, 12; Colossians 3:5-10; Acts 17:29-31; 1 Corinthians 5:12, 13; John 6:29, 27, 35, 36, 38, 39, 63, 64; 1 Corinthians 15:3-6; Revelation 14: 6-10, 12, 13; Titus 2: 11-13; Ephesians 2:13; John 14:26; Ephesians 4:10-13, John 7:16-19; 1 Corinthians 13:6-13; John 17:6-10; 1 Corinthians 14:31, 33-35, 27-30, 40; Philipians 4:4-9; John 17: 15, 20, 21; Philemon 6; 2 Corinthians 2:15, 16; 3:6, 3; 4:13, 8, 9, 18, 4-7; Romans 6:5, 8; 5:1-5; Ephesians 3:10-13, 16; 1 Peter 3:15, 16.

Matthew

Since we have these promises, dear friends, let us purify ourselves from everything that contaminates body and spirit, perfecting holiness out of reverence for God. Make room for us in your hearts. We have wronged no-one, we have corrupted no-one, we have exploited no-one. I do not say this to condemn you; I have said before that you have such a place in our hearts that we would live or die with you. I have great confidence in you; I take great pride in you. I am greatly encouraged; in all our troubles my joy knows no bounds. For when we came into Macedonia, this body of ours had no rest, but we were harassed at every turn conflict on the outside, fears within. But God, who comforts the downcast, comforted us by the coming of Titus, and not only by his coming but also by the comfort you had given him. He told us about your longing for me, your deep sorrow, your ardent concern for me, so that my joy was greater than ever. Even if I caused you sorrow by my letter, I do not regret it. Though I did regret it, I see that my letter hurt you, but only for a little while, yet now I am happy, not because you were made sorry, but because your sorrow led you to repentance. For you became sorrowful as God intended and so were not harmed in any way by us. Godly sorrow brings repentance that leads to salvation and leaves no regret, but worldly sorrow brings death.

2 Corinthians 7:1–10 NIV

THE TABERNACLE

Every first of the month, we hold by
faith the tabernacle to say thank
you and to call the presence of the
Lord Jesus Christ.
Our faith is that this brings
healing, joy, and all that the Holy
Spirit reveals to those of faith.

God bless you in the name of Jesus,
our Saviour.

Andrew

OPINION ON THIS QUESTION
by J. Fecunda

Why do you not have an organisation or a pastor of the church to send you or to guide you? Or to whom do you submit?

First of all, our organisation is the Kingdom of God by faith, belief, and conduct of life in our Master, Jesus. He's our Shepherd. We believers have one pastor, and that is Jesus. *Who guides me?* The Spirit of God, like it's written in the Bible: 'And the Spirit of God was hovering over the waters' (Genesis 1:1–2 NIV). *To whom do we submit?* To the Holy Spirit. 'But God has revealed it to us by His Spirit. The Spirit searches all things of God' (1 Corinthians 2:10 NIV). 'Moreover, we have all had human fathers who disciplined us, and we respected them for it, how much more should we submit to the Father of our Spirit and Live!' (Hebrews 12:9 NIV).

Why do you believe in God? Because of my personal relationship with Him in me! I'm forty years old and have done my share of questioning and seeking and doing. There are many theories, sciences, and concepts of which if you choose one of them, you'll have to believe! Right, so when I do my homework or research, I will still have to believe. So, God proved to be the choice for me! That's why I believe in God, for God is in me. How much of God? Depends on me becoming more and more conscious of God in me, and Jesus opened this up more when I learned more about Him.

What do you think of the churches? What about churches? Is God in churches? Yes, Genesis 3:22 NIV teaches us believers that God created man, 'And now the man has become like one of us.' I would ask, how much of God? So, this is why I would say yes, and I would emphasise and ask *how much of God is in us*, for the Scriptures also teach us that there is also evil in us. A quote from the Bible says, 'Knowing good and evil' (Genesis 3:22). The ministry God gave me through faith is what is being portrayed in this magazine, which is not funded, and the seven letters that I was inspired through faith in Jesus to write to the churches. The manifold wisdom of God should be made known to the rulers and authorities in the heavenly realms according to His eternal purpose, which He accomplished in Christ Jesus our Lord. In Him and through Him, we may approach God with freedom and confidence (Ephesians 3:10–12). All I hope to do is to fulfil this task of faith according to the grace given to do this and to speak this which is given to me by the growth of the Spirit that guides to honour and praise Jesus Christ.

I hope you realise that Jesus, in all His doings and miracles, said 'You are healed. Go!' or 'Your faith has healed you!' So really, all this is about is filling the church benches and saying we are there to congregate. It is something we are doing to avoid responsibility while not learning to give Jesus the glory and praise by becoming clear, clean, and conscious of the Holy Spirit of Jesus, which equates to love. And then we blame the man called the pastor. Remember, Jesus is personal and universal—omnipotent. He said in the book of Mark 10:45 NIV, 'For even the Son of Man did not come to be served, but to serve and to give His life as a ransom for many.' So let us know this: seek His kingdom—which is light, not darkness—with a conscious mind. We can't blame the leaders of the church (pastors), for we are responsible and should confront them with our purity and conscious mind with the love of Christ Jesus. Don't forget that God will judge us all! Amen!

My testimony is that God is true to those who seek Him honestly and earnestly will know Jesus. Like it's written in the Bible, for the sin of one man, there is reconciliation through one man, and that is Jesus (Romans 5:17). I had had a rebirth in a period where I needed guidance to the right way! So, through a friend, I was brought closer to a believers' congregation, where after a few visits, I accepted the Spirit of Jesus, which then set me apart for the growth and ministry I now have through faith and grace. I'm held strong in Christ Jesus. I say when the Spirit of Jesus is guiding, you'll know by your daily walk. You become conscious of what is of God or of the world. Repent and live. Glory to Jesus. 'For I take no pleasure in death of anyone, declares the Sovereign Lord, repent and live!' (Ezekiel 18:32 NIV). So, I thank You, Jesus.

Thomas

NEWS FROM THE BIBLE

For I do not want you to be ignorant of the fact, brothers, that our forefathers were all under the cloud and that they all passed through the sea. They were all baptised into Moses in the cloud and in the sea. They all ate the same spiritual food and drank the same spiritual drink; for they drank from the spiritual rock that accompanied them, and that rock was Christ. Nevertheless, God was not pleased with most of them; their bodies were scattered over the desert. Now these things occurred as examples to keep us from setting our hearts on evil things as they did. Do not be idolaters, as some of them were; as it is written: 'The people sat down to eat and drink and got up to indulge in pagan revelry.' We should not commit sexual immorality, as some of them did and in one day twenty-three thousands of them died. We should not test the Lord, as some of them did and were killed by snakes. And do not grumble, as some did and were killed by the destroying angel. These things happened to them as examples and were written down as warnings for us, on whom the fulfilment of the ages has come. So, if you think you are standing firm, be careful that you don't fall! No temptation has seized you except what is common to man. And God is faithful; he will not let you be tempted beyond what you can bear. But when you are tempted, he will also provide a way out so that you can stand up under it. Therefore, my dear friends, flee from idolatry. I speak to sensible people; judge for yourselves what I say. Is not the cup of thanksgiving for which we give thanks a participation in the blood of Christ? And is not the bread that we break a participation in the body of Christ? Because there is one loaf, we, who are many, are one body, for we all partake of the one loaf. Consider the people of Israel: Do not those who eat the sacrifices participate in the altar? Do I mean then that a sacrifice offered to an idol is anything, or that an idol is anything?

No, but the sacrifices of pagans are offered to demons, not to God, and I do not want you be participants with demons. You cannot drink the cup of the Lord and the cup of demons too; you cannot have a part in both the Lord's table and the table of demons. Are we trying to arouse the Lord's jealousy? Are we stronger than he? Everything is permissible but not everything is beneficial. Everything is permissible but not everything is constructive. Nobody should seek his own good, but the good of others. Eat anything sold in the meat market without raising questions of conscience, for, the earth is the Lord's, and everything in it. If some unbeliever invites you to a meal and you want to go, eat whatever is put before you without raising questions of conscience. But if anyone says to you, 'This has been offered in sacrifice', then do not eat it, both for the sake of the man who told you and for conscience' sake, for the earth is the Lord's and everything in it, the other man's conscience, I mean, not yours. For why should my freedom be judged by another's conscience? If I take part in the meal with thankfulness, why am I denounced because of something I thank God for? So, whether you eat or drink or whatever you do, do it all for the glory of God. Do not cause anyone to stumble, whether Jews, Greeks or the church of God even as I try to please everybody in every way. For I am not seeking my own good but the good of many, so that they may be saved.

1 Corinthians 10 NIV

Peter

OPEN LETTER TO PASTOR RICK JOHNSTON
12/03/02

To Pastor Mr Rick Johnston,

A graceful greeting in Christ Jesus. I know in writing this letter, we may be one in the body of Christ, our Saviour. I take pride in the ministry I have, so when invited for a visit, even a simple invitation, I'm to address the pastor and let him know of this.

We are of the Christian faith, although not under any pastor or organisation. We proclaim Jesus! My rebirth was in the Christian church Maranatha Ministries in Holland, but shortly after this, I was set apart for the ministry I'm responsible and held accountable before God, with the guidance of the Holy Spirit.

This all came about through our visit to the hospital Queen Charlotte, date 12/03/02. When questioning my wife, Veneranda, on certain issues that involves her, her answer led to explaining our faith! Midwife asking than was given info on our faith in Christ Jesus, which led to what we consider the grace of the Spirit by authority. I then gave the midwife Jacky a *Yes, We Believe Magazine*, a cassette tape, and a CD.

We are a non-funded organisation, but God provides. This is how we are held strong in the faith (Romans 1:16–17). May this testimony bless your congregation. To the glory and praise of God and consciousness of Jesus, our Saviour!

Find an enclosed copy of *Yes, We Believe Magazine*, one cassette tape, and one CD.

We hope that with your discernment as leader and pastor, we will then be invited formally by grace when this is the will of our Lord Jesus. Until then, do mention us in your prayers as we will do the same for you!

James

MY TRUTH ABOUT MY CHRISTIAN LIFE
by J. Fecunda

You may say I'm a dreamer, but I'm not the only one! This was how my testimony started which took place on the first of July 2002 on the day we celebrated the tabernacle to say thank you to God Almighty and call upon the name of Jesus Christ for us believers. The place where we praised and glorified Jesus' holy name was marked with many signs, and among them was this encouragement of peace by J. Lennon: 'Imagine all the people living life in peace.' Not only was this so, but there was recent news that we could share. I'm sure of God doing all this for the readers. Why? Because I'm just so simple in my doing that God is providing for the faith, we have in Him, the Son, and the Holy Spirit.

I had to changed my passport, and there at the location was this paper, like a newsletter, that took my attention. I understood the written text, so I took one with me. After reading it, I was filled with joy to know that our prayers of faith were answered in this testimony of Mr. Gerard van Es of the Dutch Church, Austin Friars. He wrote something in their newsletter that coincided with our faith. Only we knew or understood that it was written in 1 John 2:15–17 NIV, 'Do not love the world or anything in the world. If anyone loves the world, the love of the Father is not in him. For everything in the world, the cravings of sinful man, the lust of his eyes and the boasting of what he has and does, comes not from the Father but from the world. The world and its desires pass away, but the man who does the will of God lives for ever.'

In his story, Mr. G. van Es ends with, that in this hectic place, the words of the song 'Imagine' by J. Lennon was a good idea placed in Piccadilly Circus. Okay, I know he reads the Scriptures, and I'm sure he reads and knows this of 1 John 2:15. Only I'm not from any denomination and have a spiritual calling, so I will say my truth, and it will be based on how we just don't write the quotes of the One who really said everything, like 'I came so you can have abundant life.' Let us not imagine this but believe it, and Jesus also said in John 1:51 NIV, 'I tell you the truth, you shall see heaven open, and the angels of God ascending and descending on the Son of Man.' In Mark 13:5 NIV, Jesus said to them, 'Watch out that no one deceives you.'

I believe in Jesus, and I know he does too. However, it's a shame really that again, out of all goodness done, it's the love of Yoko Ono for John Lennon's work that is portrayed and not powerful words such as what Jesus said! I will pray, said Jesus, not for the world but for those who will remain in the world that they are protected from the evil one (John 17:15). Hey, John Lennon had the name of an apostle of the Lord Jesus. May the Lord show him mercy. I have not known him but pray in the name of Jesus for this.

To the people this story would reach, I say I'm aware also that Mr. G. van Es might have some observations as he quoted what Mr. J. Lennon had and critique on religion and that in his eyes, religion was an obstacle in this imaginary peace! Mr van Es said that religion would have to give more room for this to occur. I hope that our writing would say just this to him. He is of a religion, and we believe religion is practised by everyone who breaths air (religiously we breath air or else we'll die). Whether they are humble or egoistic or arrogant is the question. We believe in Jesus just like him and will hope to see his start of accepting us, with love for being Christians without organisation or denomination, but one in Christ Jesus by the Spirit and blood. Yoko Ono's faith is clearly in her husband's good intention of imagining peace, and she is doing something for this. It's written in Matthew 5:9, 'Blessed are the peacemakers, for they will be called sons of God.' The question is, How come out of all millions and millions of Christians, something like this positive affirmation is not set up by them and us? Something like this, for example: 'Christianity unite and stop fighting one another. Submit to Jesus!' I hope someday you will join us! There is only one God and Jesus, the mediator of God and man!

John

THE TABERNACLE

Every first of the month, we hold by faith the tabernacle to say thank you and to call the presence of the Lord Jesus Christ. Our faith is that this brings healing, joy, and all that the Holy Spirit reveals to those of faith. We started the tabernacle on the first January 2002 by the guidance of the Holy Spirit, and every first of the month, the tabernacle continues with joy, sacrifice, and prayer. This day is for us—the Tabernacle's Day, a day of the feast. In the same day, our *Yes, We Believe Magazine* came out! Every month, we can see our faith and conscience in Jesus and His kingdom is growing.

I started my walk of faith and my life's conscience of Jesus three years ago when I met my husband. I believed already in Jesus as the Son of God and Saviour, but I did not know many things about the conscience of Jesus. Now when I look at my old self, I am so happy to see the growth in myself and also the presence of the Holy Spirit every day in my life. I know the way is very long and narrow is the door as Jesus said to His disciples (Luke 13:24–27 GNT). Do your best to go in through the narrow door, because many people will surely try to go in but will not be able to.

The master of the house will get up and close the door, then you stand outside and begin to knock on the door and say, 'Open the door for us, sir!' He will answer you, 'I don't know where you came from!' Then you will answer, 'We ate and drank with you. You taught in our town!' But he will say again, 'I don't know where you came from. Get away from me, all you wicked people.' And I cannot say, 'Oh, now I know Jesus, so I'm okay.' I have to continue with constancy my walk of faith and conscience. I cannot stop because I'm conscious as well that the evil is not only outside but is also in me, and if I don't check my conduct every day, I can fall in his evil plan. For evil, I mean our ego, which needs to be in submission to the Spirit of Christ Jesus after our conscience of rebirth of the Spirit and water.

When Nicodemus asked Jesus, 'How can a grown man be born again?' Jesus replied, 'I'm telling you the truth, no one can see the kingdom of God without being born of water and the Spirit' (John 3:4–5 GNT). And in Romans 6:1–14 GNT, it's written, 'What shall we say, then? Should we continue to live in sin so that God's grace will increase? Certainly not! We have died to sin, how then can we go on living in it? For surely you know that when we were baptised into union with Christ Jesus, we were baptised into union with his death. By our baptism, then, we were buried with him and shared his death, in order that, just as Christ was raised from death by the glorious power of the Father, so also we might live a new life. For since we have become one with him in dying as he did, in the same way we shall be one with him by being raised to life as he was. And we know that our old being has been put to death with Christ on his cross, in order that the power of the sinful self might be destroyed, so that we should no longer be the slaves of sin. For when people die, they are set free from the power of sin. Since we have died with Christ, we believe that we will also live with him. For we know that Christ has been raised from death and will never die again, death will no longer rule over him. And so, because he died, sin has no power in him; and now he lives his life in fellowship with God. In the same way you are to think of yourselves as dead, so far as sin is concerned, but living in fellowship with God through Christ Jesus. Sin must no longer rule in your mortal bodies, so that you obey the desires of your natural self. Nor must you surrender any part of yourselves to sin to be used for wicked purposes. Instead, give yourselves to God, as those who have been brought from death to life, and surrender your whole being to him to be used for righteous purposes. Sin must not be your master; for you do not live under law but under God's grace.'

I remember when I met my husband, he told me, 'I can say that we are like a river. If the river stops his course, it starts to smell. The same is for us people. We cannot stop if we don't want to smell.' Our faith, our tabernacle, our magazine, our daughter, we ourselves are growing for the grace of Almighty God. We can see His presence in our life every day, and in every single day, we can see miracles. Thank You, Lord, for everything you did and are doing for us. We love You, Jesus.

MY TRUTH ABOUT MY CHRISTIAN LIFE
by V. Fecunda

In the *Yes, We Believe Magazine* of April, I asked myself and the readers, why every church or every organisation (because there are many different nominations under the name Christian) think that they are the right place for the salvation of the souls? We do not appertain to any organisation, we are Christians, and we can congregate with all Christians Believers. We have been in many different churches, here in London as well as in many other countries like Italy, Germany, Holland, France, Spain, Portugal, Israel, U.S.A., Curacao (Netherland Antilles) and I can say that in every place we have been, the Christians brothers cannot understand why we are only Christians. Often, they did not accept us because we are not under their nomination. Is it not enough to follow Jesus? We need really of a nomination. I never found in the Bible one of the many nominations that we have now, I found only the Christian Faith. In Romans 10: 13 NIV is written: "Everyone who calls on the name of the Lord will be saved." And in Mark 9: 38-40 NIV "Teacher, we saw a man driving out demons in your name and we told him to stop, because he was not one of us." "Do not stop him," Jesus said. "No one who does a miracle in my name can in the next moment say anything bad about me, for whoever is not against us is for us." Jesus did not say to his disciples "Well done, this man must follow us." So, why?................

My answer is that in every church, the leaders are led by their ego. Consequently, the congregation becomes conscience of egoism, an egoism that is hidden behind the different Christian denominations. It seems that the name of Jesus is not glorified but the name of their churches. Often this is their motto: 'To win new souls' for what? For the kingdom of God or for themselves? Before I was very angry about these things. My husband said to me, 'Hey, you cannot be angry. Anger is not from God, under the New Covenant.' Colossians 3:8 NIV states, 'But now you must rid yourselves of all such things as these: anger, rage, malice, slander and filthy language from your lips.' And he showed me again this verse of Revelation 22:11 NIV, 'Let him who does wrong continue to do wrong; let him who is vile continue to be vile let him who does right continue to do right, and let him who is holy continue to be holy.' So, what can I say? I pray that I can *love* more my Christian brothers and sisters, and I can understand more their ignorance. The sheep follow the pastor, as Jesus said. So, ask yourself, who is your pastor?

We know of a lot of wrongs done in Jesus' name, so today, just be encouraged by this love we share. Glory to Jesus. Amen.

Bartholomew

OUR JOURNEY WITH JESUS
by V. Fecunda

Dear Sarah,

I like this topic because in writing you, I remember and consider many of the blessings that God Almighty gave me so I can share with you the beautiful things and the people we met in this wonderful journey with Spirit of Christ Jesus, our Saviour, and Master. This time I will speak to you about a person you know very well, your father. Yes, your father, Mr. Jorge M. Fecunda, a man who defines himself a servant of God Almighty and whom we consider the leader and head of our family. He is a simple man with a big *faith* in Christ, and through his faith now, we are a family, a nation under the blood of Christ Jesus, as he says. He left Curaçao on May 1999 without knowing what God had in store for him. He believed, and with a small bag and a guitar, he left the island. As Jesus said to His disciples: 'Go and preach the Gospel, I will be with you.'

I met him the first time in September 1999, and God united us one month later. Often I thought, *If this man did not listen to the guidance of God, now I could not have the life I live now.* When I said this to him, he said, 'It's your faith that brought you here where you are now.' I saw many miracles in our life. I don't speak so much about him, but this month I felt the necessity to say something about this man who to me is a true servant of Christ Jesus. And often, the people are not open to understand his ministry because he is not under a church or denomination or pastor (do you remember the story of Paul per example in the Bible?). I want to speak about your father to you because I know him, and I'm not glorifying the man but the power of God Almighty that worked through a man with a big faith like your father. I want to say,

'Thank You, Jesus, for this man, for his faith in You, and for Your anointing on him.'

Dear Sarah, in this topic called 'Our Journey with Jesus,' I wrote and spoke already. And I will continue to do this (God willing) about the people whom we met; the miracles, testimonies, and challenges we had been through in this journey of life; and the stories we had in this journey of life and the stories I'm writing to you. And I thank Jesus that this time, I could write to you the true love I have for your father. I cannot remember only the beautiful things I saw in other people and forget the love I saw in him. Thank You, Jesus.

With love in Christ,

Veneranda Fecunda

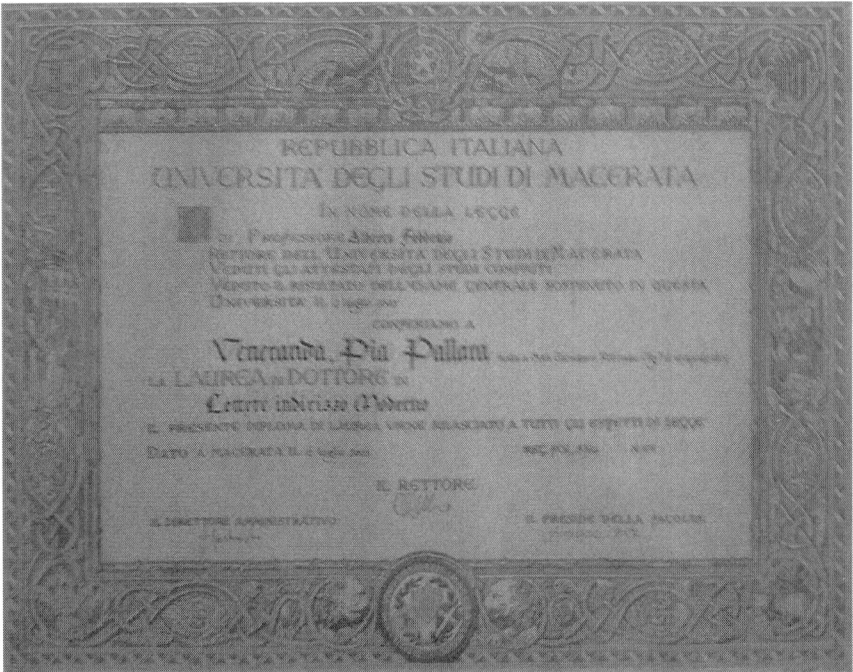

The University certificate of Vera

A collage of photos created by the kids of Vera

Vera and the family

Vera and the family after Jorge's departure

Vera and the family

Vera's Mother and Father   Jorge's Mother

Ilaria and Vera. How can you forget her big and wonderful smile?!

Vera's Pablo

Thank you for sharing your life with us! 23rd August 2018 RIP

Vera walking on the beach

Vera's brother and sister

Vera's mother, nephews, cousin, brother and kids

https://www.facebook.com/vera201
https://www.facebook.com/BwithGJorge
https://youtu.be/h8FPu2bounI
https://youtu.be/g3SHXVEjw0U
https://youtu.be/zr1qTXOMB9A
https://soundcloud.com/greatfullness/viriato-muata-feat-jorge
https://soundcloud.com/greatfullness/jesus-the-reason-for-the
https://soundcloud.com/greatfullness/belive-guitar-version

What is Faith?

"Now faith is the substance of things hoped for, the evidence of things not seen" Hebrews 11:1. Faith is the connecting power into the spiritual realm, which links us with God and makes Him become a tangible reality to the sense perceptions of a person. Faith is the basic ingredient to begin a relationship with God.

Printed and bound by CPI Group (UK) Ltd, Croydon, CR0 4YY